Wicca Candle Magic

Harness The Elementary Forces Of Fire And Discover The Secrets Of Powerful Candle Spells And Forbidden Black Magic

Arin Corvinus

Wicca Candle Magic:
Harness The Elementary Forces Of Fire And Discover The Secrets Of Powerful Candle Spells And Forbidden Black Magic

Table of Contents

Introduction

Fire has been a part of humankind for ages. We have evolved to have access to fire. Our intestines and guts have developed to process and digest cooked foods and meats that are easily processed by the gut. We have expanded across the world, into several ecosystems that our bare bodies would not be able to sustain, such as in the Arctic or far north. Most people would not survive long in Canada without any clothing or fire, for example. We lack fur and fat to keep us warm. We need fire to survive through this cold.

With the use of fire for warmth came the use of fire for protection as well. It shielded humans. It literally shielded them around the campfire, keeping wild animals at bay, so they were able to live and sleep on the ground rather than continuing to climb into trees. It protected humans from literal death.

Of course, we have come to revere the beauty in the destructive flame that every other animal has come to fear naturally. If you have ever seen a young child near a candle, you know that the child is interested in the flickering of the light—the mesmerizing way the flame seems to dance as it burns. We feel an inherent draw to its life-giving warmth, and to it, we give thanks. It is considered sacred in essentially every single culture in humanity, belonging to the Gods until someone or something stole it away to provide it to humans.

We now honor the beautiful flames ourselves, using candles to really draw ourselves closer to its beauty and strength. We allow ourselves to draw from it, not only using it in several aspects of our technology but also spiritually as well. There is something inherently cleansing about burning a candle, and Wiccans know this well.

When I was younger, we had candles everywhere throughout our home. My mother *loved* them. Of course, I had to learn the hard way about the harsh pain that can come from the bite of a flame, and yet it never killed my fascination with the flicker of light. I was taught from an early age how to honor that flame, recognizing that while it is harmful and may hurt me if I am not careful with it, there is also great energy in harnessing it as well.

In Wicca, you can literally harness the energy of the flames. You can use a candle to guide your magic, ensuring that you imbue your intentions straight through the candle as the candle burns, and in doing so, you can imagine the purification that comes along with it. You can visualize the candle burning, and as it burns, you get a physical confirmation of your energy going out into the world, so to speak. You can imagine your intentions burning into the universe as the candle melts them away.

You can imagine your candle directing your ability to purify your thoughts and your home. You can use candles to allow you to represent other people and Deities or spirits during your rituals.

The usage of candles in Wiccan magic is nearly limitless- it can be used as a tool, as a purifier, as a magnifier, or even as a way to set the ambiance for you. All you have to do is choose the best way to use it for you.

As you read through this book, you will be provided with plenty of information about using candles in the Wiccan tradition. You will effectively get a crash-course into fire and how it has shaped humans. You will see how fire has influenced mythology, as well as just how important the destructive and creative element can be. You will learn all about why you should learn how to tap into its energy, and you will be provided with several ways of doing exactly that.

You will learn about the differences in candles, colors of candles, and how to choose them. You will discover insights on how to prepare and consecrate your candles, so you know they are being used for the right purpose. You will hear about plenty of background information before learning how to put it to use.

Throughout this book, you will be given several actionable spells in several categories. You will discover love spells and money spells. You will learn how to purify and protect yourself. You will find how to how attract good luck and how to expel bad luck. You will even learn how to use certain Black Magic spells.

At the end of the day, learning how to utilize the magic of candles, one of the most fundamental tools in the Wiccan way of life, will be a game-changer for you. In learning to use this tool, you will be able to communicate with the universe around you, employing the tiny flame to send out your intentions and help you keep your mind focused.

Chapter 1: Unveiling The Elementary Forces Of Fire

Fire is almost hypnotic. Have you ever sat and stared into the flickering of a candle's flame or the crackling of a campfire? It is one of the four elements within Wicca, along with the earth, the air, and water, and it is the only one that will immediately harm the body when directly touched. Nevertheless, it is almost essential to us as humans. Particularly early humans, who did survive without it for a period of time, saw huge benefits to wielding this deadly beautiful element for the first time in history. It allows for cooking, for light, and to stay warm. Humans do not have the fur to keep warm that other animals do. Instead, we rely on the warmth of the flames to keep us alive and well overnight.

This power, despite how beautiful and useful it is, or how manageable it can be when controlled, can quickly become out of control. It has a power of its own, and if not managed properly, there is nothing stopping a small candle from turning into a devastating house fire, or a campfire from burning down an entire mountainside.

It is this particular power that makes fire so fascinating and worthy of reverence to so many people. It gives life and helps us live, but at the same time, it reminds us that it can destroy and take away just as quickly as it gives that life. Fire, despite the fact that it can be quelled by any of the other three elements, can also consume those elements instead of being destroyed by them. It burns away at oxygen in the air. It eats wood from the Earth. Its temperatures evaporate the water. It destroys, but as it does so, it also primes the area and earth for rebirth as well. In fact, certain trees' seeds require the heat from the flames to open up and allow for the growth of new ones. It is so volatile, so powerful, so nurturing, and so destructive, all wrapped up into one elemental package, and that balance between gentle nourishment and utter destruction and devastation is beautiful and worthy of being honored.

Fire In History

Fire itself is incredibly important, as established— and humans have managed to tame it, to an extent. Flames, which were once associated with fear and destruction, became an essential tool for survival and the continual development of humankind. It is believed to have first been utilized and controlled starting back with *Homo erectus,* one of the earlier species of humans. There have been traces found that root back the first use of fire by humankind as being 1,000,000 years ago.

With the discovery of fire and managing to utilize it, humans suddenly had a source of warmth and an ability to cook. Humans, then, could begin to migrate into colder temperatures. They no longer had to worry about their delicate, furless bodies freezing in the colder climates, thanks to their ability to sue fire to stay warm and survive, even through colder nights.

It did more than just keep them warm; however, humans were able to then protect themselves at night. The vast majority of the animal world inherently fears the awesomely destructive powers of fire, recognizing just how dangerous it is and can be. This means that they will avoid the flames, therefore avoiding the humans using it as a sort of shield. They could light a fire within a cave, and other animals would clear out, instinctively fleeing from the flames in an attempt at self-preservation.

This is the beginning of fire as a protector—it shielded these humans from being hunted at night, and it kept them enveloped in warmth. It helped nourish them. They discovered that cooking food allowed humans to easier consume meat, and with more meat came more caloric intake. They could dry meat through the use of fire to keep it from rotting and expiring, which then meant that food could be preserved and saved for future use with ease.

Even larger fires became useful for humans. They could burn downloads to clean the space, allowing for the land to grow more crops, as well as making hunting simpler as more of the brush or other hiding places that their prey may have hidden underneath was banished. This usage of fire then allowed for the separation of tasks in society, allowing for some people to be the hunters while others were tasked with the preparation and preservation of food.

The longer people had fire within their grasp to use as a tool, the more influential it became. They discovered how to use flames to harden their weapons and spears, making sure that they were more durable and effective. This then allowed for the changing of hunting methods. As the spears became hardened, they could become thrust into other animals, rather than having to throw them to build up any sort of momentum they would need to properly penetrate. This then means that they could stalk and ambush prey instead, waiting in brush before leaping into action. Beyond just that, evidence has been found of humans using flames to heat rocks that then became shaped into the arrowheads and blades that were used to process the meat.

Of course, as humans no longer had to fight so hard for their survival, gaining the tools that would set them apart from other species, they were able to begin focusing on other sorts of activities, such as art. With more time freed up because they had more efficient methods of hunting, protecting, and eating, they were able to dedicate their time to tasks that were considered pleasurable instead of necessary for survival. This brought the use of fire into art. Several statues have been found to be created with ivory, while others were made of clay that had been fired. Something that is still used today. These ceramics began being used during the

Neolithic Age, and over time, that ceramic work became more intricate.

All of this compounded upon itself, and humans were able to begin evolving at rapid paces, developing all of the necessary criteria to begin diversifying their skills. With fire and tools came the ability to begin planting crops or building shelter. The brain could grow larger thanks to the higher level of nourishment. Because hunting became easier, more meat could be consumed, providing humans with more protein, and with the use of flames, inventions and discoveries were spurred. Humans no longer had to sleep in the trees to avoid predators and instead were able to sleep on the ground around a fire. They were safe, and they were nourished—thanks to the fire.

Fire In Mythology

With the prevalence of fire in nearly every aspect of human life, it comes as no surprise that humans began using fire in their mythology as well. Ancient Greeks told the story of Prometheus, the titan who loved humans and chose to defy the gods to deliver fire to man. He, in particular, was regarded as having stolen power and skills from the gods Zeus, Hephaestus, and Athena, granting them all to mankind, despite Zeus's reservations and suffered for an eternity after doing so.

In Cherokee legend, there is Grandmother Spider.She stole fire away from the sun and gave it to humans so we could see through the darkness that originally enveloped the world. She captured the light in her bowl of clay and brought light from the west to the east, bringing the sun, light, and fire to humankind and allowing for survival.

In several different cultures, you can see a pattern. Fire was a tool of the Gods, something for humanity to desire and pine over, but not something that was granted to them until it was stolen away. It was not discovered but rather given as a gift from some sort of spirit or god that pitied humans and wanted them to have the best possible life—and the development of controlling fire absolutely provided that for us.

Across cultures, there are Gods and Goddesses associated with the flames. You can see the Celtic Brighid and Bel, both of whom rule over fire. In Greek mythology, Hephaestus controlled flames and the forge, allowing for the wielding of fire to create. Hestia guarded the Hearth, bringing warmth to humans within their homes and allowing them to survive in the cold while remaining under her warm protection from wild animals. In ancient Rome, Vesta and Vulcan ruled over flames and volcanoes—one of the most potent forms of fire on the planet. You can see flames revered in Hawaii, with Pele being associated with volcanoes in general.

Role Of Fire In The Wiccan Tradition

Fire itself is associated primarily with masculine energy. Wicca itself is seen as a sort of balance between the masculine and feminine, between the

God and Goddess who come together as the Mother and Father of our planet. These Deities nurture us, like two sides to the same sort of power, and fire, in particular, is associated with the God, reminiscent of the burning energy of the Sun that bathes our planet in energy that gives us life.

When tapping into the element of fire, you will primarily be using candles—and this is the focus of much of the book. Remember, as always, when you are working with fire, take the time to take special care—the flames can very quickly spiral out of control, burning and destroying if you are not careful with them.

When you are using fire, you should always make sure that you take the proper precautions. Make sure your flame is not surrounded by anything flammable, and that you keep the flames contained into something that will not burn if the candle tips for any reason. Many people, when they are burning candles or items, prefer to place their candles and flames inside a cauldron to contain the flames. Even if the candle tips, the cauldron should not catch fire, unless the candle was floating in oils (but please do not do this!).

Fire is associated with life itself, making it a direct link to the Gods and their energy. It drives our passion, our ability to create, but also the destructive portion of the cycle of life and death. It is good and bad—it is life-saving and life-threatening. It is powerful, and that makes it particularly worthy of being treated with the reverence it commands.

The Wiccan Element Of Fire

When using fire in Wicca, there are two major ways to do so. You can use it in ritual, and you can use it in magic, and both of these will work their ways into several of the spells and rituals you will go through the process of learning to cast as you continue to learn about the Wiccan way of life. It can be used to light candles, to burn sage, or to burn other items or objects as well. Depending on the way it is used, it can symbolize various different aspects or ways of life, and when you use it in ritual or magic, you can use it for several correspondences.

Fire In Ritual

When using fire in ritual, it is usually called from the sough—this means that in a circle that has been cast, fire will primarily be placed on the southernmost point, though you can really call it from any direction that you feel is appropriate. Remember, Wicca is not an exact science that requires precision and mimicry—you can use it in any way that it calls to you. You should always choose to follow your intuition—that gut feeling you get when the universe's energy is attempting to guide you. For some people, they call fire from the direction of the sun, meaning that those who are north of the equator will see fire as coming from the south, while those in the southern hemispheres will see it as more of a northern energy.

When utilizing fire in ritual, the most common ways to do so are through lighting candles or through using items that are representative of fire, such as the wand or the blade. Because fire is not always safe to light in certain situations, an individual may choose to instead place an item that is representative of the flames upon their altar for ritual instead, but when it is possible, others will use legitimate flames, such as a bonfire.

Fire In Magic

The element of fire gets evoked in several different spells, particularly when they are related to any of the particular powers and correspondences of fire to begin with, such as energy or sexuality. The element of fire can be utilized in several of these different spells, ranging from anything from protection to transformation. Here is a list of several of the types of spells that may utilize this element in some way:

- Sexuality, passion, love, energy, the family

- Authority, power, destruction, courage, will, strength, exercise
- Innovation, invention, enthusiasm, loyalty, vision, transformation, kitchen magic
- Protection, healing, purification

It is frequently used in ceremonies, allowing the use of fire to activate various other ingredients that are being used. It can be used to burn, allowing you to release your intentions and energy into the universe, and through burning, you can also create offerings to the Gods and Goddesses. It can be used to burn incense, allowing for the activation of the air element.

Fire's Correspondences

Fire itself can be used with several different correspondences, all of which are related in some way to the energy of fire, which itself is active, masculine, and dry. Usually, on an altar, it is represented with either a bowl for fire, a candle, or a blade of some sort.

- **Season:** Summer
- **Day:** Sunday
- **Moon phase:** The Waxing Moon
- **Time of day:** Noon
- **Symbol:** A triangle with the point going upwards
- **Tools:** The wand, athame (a-tha-may), dagger, burned paper or herbs, candles, fire in general
- **Spirits:** Djinn, Sprites, and Salamanders
- **Animals:** Squirrel, phoenix, ram, scorpion, mantis, fox, salamander, dragon, lion, snake, coyote
- **Herbs:** Seeds and nuts, tobacco, cinnamon, almond trees, poppy, thistles, onion, garlic, juniper, hibiscus, allspice, nettles, basil, chili, cactus, mustard
- **Fragrances:** Chamomile, bay, patchouli, clove
- **Incense:** Dragon's blood, cinnamon, or frankincense

- **Sabbats:** Samhain, Midsummer, Lughnasadh, and Beltane
- **Astrological signs:** Aries, Leo, and Sagittarius
- **Colors:** Maroon, crimson, fuchsia, scarlet, gold, orange, white, and red
- **Gods and Goddesses:** Vulcan, Atar, Mars, Themis, Ra, Aetna, Agni, Yansa, Aten, Elena, Chu-Jung, Durga, Hephaestus, Vesta, Horus, Hestia, Pele, Freya, Brigit

Candles In Wiccan Ritual

Candles themselves are used in the vast majority of rituals and spells that you will encounter during your time studying Wicca. They are used around the world is far more contexts than just Wicca as well— you can find them setting the stage around the world for a wide range of rituals, providing the perfect lighting and helping purify the area.

In Wicca in particular, you use a candle and the lighting of the candle to symbolize the beginning of your ritual. The lighting is essentially the start of the ceremony, and when it burns out, or you blow it out, you end the ceremony. You can see this in other religions as well, such as the Catholic church, in which candles are lit at the beginning and blown out at the end, or in many different Pagan rituals as well.

By lighting the candle, you are honoring God—creating a sympathetic representation of the being that you are choosing to honor. You may not be able to have that particular person or Deity actively present in your room, but you can use a candle to represent them. This is commonly done in general culture as well, lighting a candle to remember your lost loved ones during important holidays.

When you are using candles yourself, you will be lighting them to represent the God or Goddess that you are attempting to communicate with—it is your way of creating a manifestation of the other person in order to let them know that you have them on your mind.

Lighting your candle should be something that is personal for you—when you do it, you have thoughtfully and carefully selected the candle that you wish to employ, and you are able to represent the individual that you are hoping to honor or create an offering for.

Even more specifically, beyond when candles are used to represent someone, they are seen to be a representation of the element of fire itself. The candle is a relatively safe way for you to actively utilize fire without it burning or destroying anything around you. You can contain the flame in a controlled setting, and in doing so, you can bring the element of fire into your ritual or spellwork, honoring the element and using it to summon its presence. Most often, it is placed on the southernmost point of your altar or circle when used in this manner.

Importance Of Candles For Magic

Considering how popular the use of the candle is in ritual, it should come as no surprise that they are used for magical purposes as well. They are not only symbolic and can be actively used in spellwork. By using the candle, you can activate its magic in several different ways. However, before you are able to activate the magic, you must first be able to pick the proper candle for you. In order to do so, you must understand what you will be attempting to convey or create. Chapter 2 will walk you through the process of selecting the right candle for the magic you have in mind.

Candles to Activate

The first way that candles can be used in magic is as an activator. Similarly, to how they are used to start a ritual, they are able to start the spell. They can bring the energy to you, or they can send it outwards as well, depending on the candle and how it has been prepared. This candle can be used to burn until it extinguishes itself, allowing it to continuously work as it is lit, or it can be relit and extinguished regularly for the duration of a spell, depending on your needs and usage.

This magic allows for the energy of the item that you are interacting with to be truly released and regulated. You essentially are lighting the candle as you allow your intention to either draw energy toward you or take that energy away, meaning it can purify and expel negativity or it can attract whatever your intention was, to begin with.

Candles to Create Sympathetic Magic

The magic can also be used to create sympathetic relationships, serving as a representation of a specific person during the spell—they can be decorated in certain ways, charged, and imbued with the right intentions and energy. They can also be carved and dressed, allowing them to better represent the individual that they are supposed to. When you are able to represent someone else, you can have them present in your spell symbolically, allowing you to perform spells on other people, even from a distance. You can do a love spell, lighting a candle to represent the other party, or you can do a spell that is intended to represent a God or Goddess, making them one of the beings privies to your spell as it happens.

Being able to use your candles to represent other people and beings allows you far more flexibility in your magical abilities—because you will be able to cast spells from a distance, inviting other people into the spell without them ever being present, you can protect yourself. You can influence others to love you or find you attractive. You can relate to several of the Gods or Goddesses that you wish to commune with or honor as you ask for their guidance and aid. You can even represent the Sun and Moon if they are relevant to your spell that is at hand.

This sympathetic magical representation, then, allows you to make anyone or anything the subject of your spell, especially if you are able to prepare your candle properly. When you prepare your candle, using a mixture of runes, dressings, herbs, or even just a piece of paper with the name of the person you are attempting to influence, you can effectively do anything you wish, sending your intentions across the entire world to the individual that you wish to influence.

Chapter 2: Selecting The Right Candles For Your Magical Practices

Before you can begin casting your spells and learning how to use candles, however, you need to start developing a solid foundation of which kind of situation and spell calls for what kind of candle. You cannot just take any candle you see and assume it will work just right. While you may be able to create some influence in doing so, the best way to truly be successful at Wiccan magic is to know when to use which tool and to use those tools to the best of their capabilities.

In this case, you want to learn how to pick the perfect candle. You can do this relatively simple, and while you may eventually get this down to memory, it may help you to take this list and transcribe it into your Book of Shadows for future reference. Doing so can provide you with a handy tool that you can reference at a glance to ensure that you are always choosing the right candle for the right job.

Candles are used in nearly every ritual and spell you will do, though there are some that require nothing more than yourself. Because of that, you will find yourself constantly needing to select candles as you go through the process of learning how to cast spells yourself. This can be intimidating. If you have ever been in a candle aisle, you know that there are several different kinds of candles in every color imaginable. Each color and each shape will have different tendencies and meanings, and if you learn how to navigate through this, learning which candles will best be used in any situation, you will be able to make sure you start each ritual and spell on the best foot that you possibly can.

Remember, candles are used representatively and to charge and begin your spell, attracting or repelling energies depending on your intention and usage. Despite how small the candle is, remember that it is incredibly powerful. It has the ability to burn down your house relatively easily if you were to knock it over or otherwise cause a problem for yourself. No matter how small it may be, it needs to be treated with the care, caution, honor, and reverence it deserves. It not only is able to pull energy around it, which adds to its utility, but it can also be quite destructive if not treated right.

Candle Types

Candles can come in nearly every shape and form—you can get candles that are shaped, that is intended to unlock chakra, that is meant to represent masculinity or femininity. Despite the fact that candles share one thing in common—they are meant to be burned—they are all quite different, and the energies that they will attract and the effects they will have can vary widely.

As you go through this process of learning about the candles, take some time to consider the situations in which you would use each and every one of them.

Table Candles

These are candles that are readily available in stores—they are usable for most rituals, especially if you go through the process of anointing and preparing them for use. When you are buying these candles, you may find that you are overwhelmed with just how many options there are, but make sure that when you do buy these, they are not dipped in anything. You want them clean and pure so you can direct their magic in any way that you see fit. These are all-purpose candles that can be in any shape and may be in a container of some sort. They are commonly used to burn at home.

Taper Candles

Unlike table candles, taper candles are a bit more delicate and specific. These will always require a candle holder because they are so narrow—they would be unstable on their own if you tried to stand them on their small base. These candles are usually quite long and thin. Thanks to their size, however, they burn quite quickly as well, meaning these are the perfect pick if you are short on time and need something that you can burn through.

Because they are so thin, they are quite delicate, and it can be easy to snap them in half, which of course, is counterproductive. You must be quite gentle with them, especially as you dress and anoint them, and especially if you need to carve into them at all. These are commonly available in colors as well, specifically for magical purposes, but when you are buying these candles, you must make sure that they have been colored all the way through rather than being white in the center and dipped into the color that they are. By ensuring that they are colored all the way through, you can ensure that they will be as effective as possible for your particular situation.

Altar, Pillar, And Jumbo Candles

All three of these candles are quite thick and tall. Thanks to their size and thickness, they take longer to burn, but that makes them particularly effective to use as an altar candle or as a candle that you dedicate to a specific Deity. You light them first and extinguish them at the end of the ritual, but you will want to reuse these as you do spells. They can be used to represent your Deity when you do not need to burn the entire candle at one time.

These can also come in candles that are in a glass container already, and they are usually known as 7-day candles—they can handle burning for extremely long periods before they are used up.

Image Candles

Image candles are designed to represent one specific person or shape, and they create a specific goal in your ritual. When you use these, they are already specifically designed to fill a role-based upon their shapes. These can come in several different forms, such as:

- **The Adam and Eve Candle:** This candle is shaped like a naked male and female together. They can come in several different colors, and because of this, they are particularly useful in spells relating to love. You can use them when you are looking at love and attractive spells, and depending on the color, and how you anoint them, they can be used to either attract a partner or send away or break up the relationship altogether.

- **The Mummy or Skull Candle:** As inferred by the name, they are shaped as either a mummy within a coffin or a skull. Despite the morbid design, they are intended to protect from danger, death, and illness. They ward away this negativity, protecting the user.

- **Cat Candle:** This candle, as you may have inferred, is shaped like a cat. The black cat can chase away bad luck, which then creates a vacuum effect that attracts good luck to you. It can be used to break any negative spells that have been cast, such as hexes and jinxes. A green cat, on the other hand, can be used to encourage prosperity and will welcome and encourage the healing of pets in particular. Red cats can be used in love spells.

- **Seven-knob Candle:** This candle is made of seven different knobs, meant for one candle per day to be lit across a week period. This is perfect when you have a weeklong spell to complete, as it is already divided up for you. These can come in several different colors, depending on what your end goal is, such as:

  o **Black:** Perfect for releasing or banishing spells
  o **Blue:** Warding off confusion, depressive episodes, and fighting
  o **Brown:** Spells of justice

- o **Green:** Manifestation spells, court case spells, or money spells
- o **Orange:** Used to remove any obstacles or create and encourage successful business
- o **Red:** Encouraging energy to move, breaking down barriers, or love spells
- o **Violet:** Protection and defense of spirit from other spiritual attacks
- o **White:** All-purpose, purification, or the granting of hidden wishes
- o **Yellow:** Removing and expelling bad luck

- **Devil-be-Gone Candle:** This candle usually takes the shape of what is recognized as the Christian devil and is used specifically in exorcisms or when a spiritual entity of any sort needs to be removed. It is especially efficient when you use it alongside an astral candle that is prepared to represent the individual that is in need of cleaning or purification.

- **Cross or Crucifix Candle:** As implied, these are in the shape of the Cross or the Crucifix, and these are perfect as an offering to the God or Goddess if you need to prepare one. Otherwise, this should be used when banishing negativity or in protection spells.

Astral Or Zodiac Candles

Astral candles are usually representative through sympathetic magic—they are meant to represent a specific person, either yourself or someone else. They are usually lined up with the individual's Zodiac sign is represented by color. These candles should always be allowed to burn to completion, or if you must put one out, you should make sure you store the candle itself in a safe place. Discarding them should not happen, especially when not entirely burnt. These can be used for most spells when you need a representation of the individual.

The colors that are used to represent each of the Zodiac signs include:

- **Aries:** Red, white, or pink
- **Taurus:** Pink, green, red, or yellow
- **Gemini:** Silver, yellow, red, or blue
- **Cancer:** White, green, or brown
- **Leo:** Orange, gold, red, or green
- **Virgo:** Yellow, black, gold, or grey
- **Libra:** Light brown, black, or blue
- **Scorpio:** Red, black, or brown
- **Sagittarius:** Blue, purple, red, or gold
- **Capricorn:** Brown, black, or red
- **Aquarius:** Green or blue
- **Pisces:** White, blue, or green

Scented Candles

Sometimes, you may choose to use scented candles. These can be useful when you need to incorporate a few extra properties into your spell for any reason, or when they are called for. When you wish to use a scented candle, you should make sure that you are always mindful of which scents you use to encourage certain magical properties or elements. Here is a chart to help you choose which scents you may wish to incorporate into your rituals and magic:

- **Vanilla:** Sexual energy, lust, or memory enhancement
- **Tangerine:** Prosperity
- **Sandalwood:** Purifies, heals, and protects
- **Strawberry:** Attracts luck, love, and friendship
- **Rose:** Attracts and encourages love
- **Pine:** Encourages strength and the elimination of negativity
- **Musk:** Encourages and attracts love and lust, as well as provides and bolsters strength and courage
- **Myrrh:** Purifies and protects
- **Patchouli:** Draws and attracts fortune and money

- **Lotus:** Attracts inner peace and encourages harmony
- **Frangipani:** Attracts positivity
- **Jasmine:** Encourages and fosters love
- **Honeysuckle:** Brings forth luck, heals, and bolsters psychic powers
- **Coconut:** Purifies and protects
- **Carnation:** Heals
- **Cherry:** Attracts and encourages love
- **Blueberry:** dispels negative energy

Candle Colors

Along with choosing out which kind of candle and what scent you may wish to use in your spells, color is another important consideration. This section will discuss the use of colors in candles, but for an easy guide, consider referring to the back of this book for the Tables of Correspondence, which will have a quick, easy to look at guide to the meaning behind each color without all of the frill, fluff, or explanation that you will see here.

Black

Black as a color is avoid—it is the absence of light on the spectrum, but the absence does not imply that it is bad. Despite the fact that it is black, consider that the color of blackness is avoid—it absorbs all colors, which is why wearing black is so uncomfortable on a hot day. It absorbs instead of reflecting, and as such, it also absorbs negativity. By absorbing the negative energy instead of allowing it to continue to flow, the negative energy around you is pulled from the air. You can use this to protect, repel, reverse, or even banish magic or energy from your surroundings. You can also use this color to remove negativity altogether, to overcome obstacles or blockages that are preventing you from moving forward, and to cause issues and promote chaos or dysfunction among your enemies.

Blue

Blue is a relaxing color by nature, and it is commonly used to heal and strengthen the mind in spell casting. You can use this to encourage sleep, for example, allowing your intention to sleep to flow into the candle before burning it for a few short minutes and putting it out. When you use a blue candle, you are encouraging one's inherent understanding and awareness of the spiritual world, and generally speaking, the shade of blue you use matters as well:

- Light blue candles tend to bring about peace, tranquility, and clarity.
- Medium shades of blue candles tend to bring spiritual strength and fortitude, as well as a deep inner peace.
- Dark blue shades tend to show deep thoughts and spirituality—these may cause moodiness if you are not careful in how you use them.

Brown

Brown candles are largely natural—it is the color of the dirt beneath your feet and many different animals. This color is usually applied with other colors as well in order to tie your spell to the natural world, influencing the world around you rather than you or someone else. Usually, you may use darker russet brown in uncertain situations, such as if you are unsure about your love life, while medium brown can symbolize some sort of pause or hesitancy to understand what is happening next.

Green

Green candles tend to represent growth, fortune, and prosperity in general, as well as the element of Earth. These candles are also related to healing, much like how the blue ones are. When you light a green candle, you are likely preparing for a spell that has some sort of tie to money, such as asking for help to get a promotion or to undertake a new financial venture. These candles can also help you achieve success in your business, whatever that business may be.

Gold

Gold candles are primarily associated with the God, the Sun, and masculinity. Often seen as the counterpart to silver, gold candles are also related primarily to finances and businesses, much like green. They are fantastic for attracting any sort of knowledge that you are in need of, as well as finding fortune, money, or developing a power of influence or healing.

Orange

Orange candles are energetic and attentive—when you use orange, you are attempting to attract something, whether that is energy, influence, intentions, or other objects in the universe. If you are trying to find someone or something that is lost, for example, you may choose to use orange candles. You can also combine the orange of this candle with others in order to be a fortifier, strengthening the intention of the other color. Overall, orange is positive spiritual and physical energy and is associated with being encouraging and allowing for clear thoughts.

Pink

Pink candles are usually indicative of some sort of connection, be it love or friendship. They are nurturing, and they encourage the art of communication. They are usually used before any sort of ceremony that will link people together or otherwise emphasize the bond between two people. This means that you will often see these during marriage ceremonies or to influence love and romance, encouraging the affection and romantic feelings.

Silver

Silver is first and foremost associated with the Goddess, the Moon and celestial bodies, and femininity. When you are using a silver candle, you are attempting to dispel any sort of negative energy that is present around you. You are encouraging good to win in its endeavor to overtake evil, and in doing so, you are able to encourage reflection and a connection to the Moon. It encourages the use of intuition, and you may use this candle if you are trying to meditate on what to do next or how best to proceed with your situation at hand.

Red

Red candles are primarily meant to convey passion and health—they are associated with energy and vitality, representing health itself. In burning a red candle, you are able to power the soul, bolstering it and allowing yourself to prevent being influenced by negativity or corruption. Along with health and passion, it is also seen frequently with lust and sexual passion, as well. Of all the colors for your candle, this is the closest one to represent the element of fire. When you use a red candle, you are filling yourself with courage—maybe you are getting ready to go into an interview, an important meeting, or even a date.

Violet

Violet candles are reminiscent of power—blue is about awareness, while violet encourages prowess in the magical world. When you use a violet candle, you are encouraging a buildup of your magic, strengthening your spells. If you are attempting to cast a love spell, for example, you may choose to burn a violet candle while also burning a pink one to really magnify the effects of the candle's affinity for love.

White

White is pure and unifying—its purity allows for it to be used in virtually any context, though it is most commonly associated with truth and illumination. It is used primarily for defensive or purifying reasons, though you can choose white when you do not have the right color that is being called for or when you feel like you are unsure which color to use. When you use white, you encourage strength and power, as well as revere innocence and purity.

It can help you connect with the spiritual world and to prevent evil from taking you over.

Yellow

Yellow candles are associated with knowledge and discovery. They are meant to improve visualization and encourage movement toward innovation. These are most strongly aligned with the element of air. When you light a yellow candle to burn with you as you study, you will find that you absorb the information better, making it particularly useful. This can range from a light yellow all the way to a bright shade of lime yellow, or even have golden undertones. It is meant to convey and represent any sort of cheerfulness or attraction, and it is used in encouraging the fulfillment of dreams.

Chapter 3: The Secrets Of Cleansing And Consecration

Selecting your candle is just the beginning. You still have to process the candle, preparing it to work for you. Think for a moment about preparing a meal—you may buy a slab of raw meat, but you would not yet serve it for dinner—you must still prepare it into something cohesive in order for it to be delicious and nutritious. Just as you will still need to trim, season, and cook your meat before serving it to your guests, you must also prepare your candle.

When you are preparing your candle, however, instead of trimming and seasoning it before cooking like you would a piece of meat, you are going to first cleanse your candle of energy and then consecrate it. Consecrating is a fancy word meaning that you will prepare and dedicate the item to being used for your divine purpose, declaring the intent to use it specifically for the purpose that you have chosen for it.

Consecrating the candle can come in several different forms, such as anointing, coating it with herbs, or carving it, and depending on your intent and the spell that you will be using, you will need to choose the method that works best for you in the moment. As you read through this chapter, you will build up an idea of when it is appropriate to use each of these methods and how best to go about the process.

This step is incredibly important. Remember that as you do this, you are preparing for your spell or ritual, and because of this, you want to do the best job you can manage. You want to ensure that you are able to make the spell as effective as possible, and that effectiveness will come with the quality of your spell, as well as intention. This means that you do not want to rush through these steps as you prepare for your spell. Instead, take the time to slowly and carefully dedicate and prepare your candles, using it as a time to really reflect upon the purpose of your spell and ensure that you will be able to complete it exactly as intended.

How To Cleanse A Candle

The first preparation you will do is cleansing your candle. When you do this, you are effectively purifying it in some way. Remember, your candle has been out in the world before it arrived in your home or on your altar. Even if you bought it new, it was still shipped to you, handled by whoever it was that manufactured the candle, and then shipped to a retailer, where it was likely placed upon shelves, or packaged and sold to you if you bought it online. It would then be handled by several people as it traveled to your location, and by the time you get it, you have no idea where it has been, how many people it has passed, or how clean or pure the area around it was. It has been handled by so many people, absorbing energy and intentions as it went, that it is incredibly important for you to go through this cleansing process.

By cleansing your candle, you will release any and all energy that has been absorbed. You essentially turn your candle into a clean slate that you will be able to use in order to make your candle far more open to the intentions that you are hoping to imbue it with for your spell. Even if you have made the candle yourself, unless you have done so just then for that specific spell, it is a good idea to cleanse it prior to the spell's completion simply to safeguard it. You do not want your spell to be tainted with any negative energy at all; instead, you want it open and accepting of all positive intentions and energy that you are attempting to project.

When trying to purify your candle, you have several options, depending on which you feel is appropriate at the time. We will discuss four effective ways that can be used to purify your candle. Ultimately, you need to pick the one that you feel works best for you.

Cotton and Alcohol

One method involves little more than a tissue or cotton ball along with rubbing alcohol. Rubbing alcohol is not only good for killing bacteria—you can use it to help you expel energy from your candle as well. Starting at the bottom of the candle, take your cotton saturated in alcohol and rub it gently. Do not scrub too hard, especially if this is a narrow candle, as you do not want to damage it. As you rub the candle gently, imagine the energy within the candle releasing. Imagine it as a flame, burning at the tip of the wick as you slowly rub along the wax, working your way up slowly. The energy will be expelled through the tip of the candle as you do so.

Purified with Sage

Another way that you can cleanse a candle is through burning sage. Sage itself is deeply intertwined with the idea of purifying a room. The smoke, as you burn it, purifies the area around you, and it is often used to purify an area during an exorcism or if negative energy is present within the setting.

When you are using sage to purify your candle, start burning the sage, or you can use a purifying incense here as well. As the sage or incense begins to smoke, hold the candle in the cloud, allowing it to soak in the purifying effects, and allowing the smoke to take out the energies, drawing them out into the smoke as it wafts away.

As you do this, imagine the energy all fading away, being pulled by the smoke, and dissipated back into the universe. The candle should be left a clean slate as your incense or sage finishes its burn, leaving you with a candle that is ready for further preparation.

Sea Salt

Salt is well-known as a preserving method—you can use it when you are attempting to sanitize or preserve food, for example. It literally protects the food from going bad as you cure the meat. However, salt also has important ties to Wiccan culture, as well. Salt is a powerful purifier, and you can use it when you are casting circles, performing spells, or even purifying your candle. When you set out to cleanse your candle, start by pouring salt into a bowl. The bowl should be large enough to accommodate the candle, and you need enough salt to bury the candle. Place the candle into the salt and bury it, covering the entire thing in salt.

When you place it into the salt, imagine the crystals of salt absorbing the negative energy, pulling them away and freeing the candle from the energy that has tainted it. You must leave the candle sitting in the salt for at least 24 hours, making this one the most timely method of cleansing a candle, but it is the least involved of all four methods. If you know that you will be performing spells ahead of time, you can do this to save yourself precious preparation time later. After 24 hours, your candle is ready to use.

Moonlight Cleanse

Particularly during the light of the Full Moon, you can cleanse items with ease. Of course, even just a little bit of Moonlight will be enough, but the effects and strength will be far stronger if you leave it out during the Full Moon. When you use this method, you are allowing the energy of the Moon to bathe the candle overnight, slowly purifying it and allowing the Moon's energy to draw out the negativity within it. This means that you can effectively cleanse the candle with no effort, so long as you leave it out overnight.

You can set your candle onto a windowsill that will be bathed in Moonlight, or you can place it outside. What is important is that the Moon's light will shine on it. The next morning, you should try to pick up your candle before the Sun's light is able to shine on it. Afterward, the candle is purified and ready for future ritual or spellwork.

How To Consecrate The Candle

With your purified candle, are prepared to consecrate your candle. This is your dedication to the purpose of the spell you are attempting to do. During this, you will fill your candle with your intention, deciding exactly what you will be doing with it and filling it with that energy. As you consecrate your candle, you will do something else with it as you think and focus your energy on it. The methods of consecrating your candle can vary from using oils and herbs to engraving it. Some people choose to use holy water or Moon water to consecrate their candle as well. The method that you use will depend on your personal preferences as well as the intention and intensity you will need for your spell.

After you consecrate your candle, you will be ready to begin your spell or ritual, which the rest of this book will focus on teaching you to do. Make sure you really understand this process, and again, do not rush through the consecration. The more entirely that you are able to imbue the candle with your intentions and desires, the more the candle will be able to deliver the results you are hoping for. Your candle will burn, and with it, it will send out the intention and energy that you have filled it in with. With the energy-burning and emanating outward into the universe, you create a gap in energy in which something else must flow in. the hope is for the energy to bring with it whatever you were attempting to obtain with your spellcasting in the first place.

Anointing And Dressing The Candle

The first method of consecration that we will discuss is anointing and dressing. This is a simple process—you are using oil to cover the candle and then potentially dressing it with herbs, which involves you covering the candle in the herbs that will help strengthen your message to the universe.

When you are going to anoint your candle, you must first choose an oil that will work for you. This oil will be related to the intention that you are hoping to send out into the universe. You want to find an oil that really lines up with the particular goals that you have in mind for your spell. See the **Table of Correspondence** at the end of this book for a list of several oils that you can use for this process as well as the traits that they line up with. You will be able to use that to determine what you will need for your spell, and then you can go out and get the proper oils.

With the oil chosen, it is time to anoint the candle—at this point, you should take the candle and close your eyes. Really imagine the goal that you are hoping to imbue into the candle, focusing on your goals and wishes that you have. Imagine those goals and wishes filling your fingers—perhaps you visualize this energy literally illuminating your fingertips. Now, dip your finger in the oil and prepare to rub it into your candle.

It is important to note that when you are anointing a candle, you want to start at the top and work your way down when you are attempting to attract something to you. This process will attract positive energies, luck, and other benefits to you. When you wish to expel something, however, you want to start at the bottom and work your way up. This direction is incredibly important, and if you can keep this in mind, you should find that you are able to send out just the right kind of energy into the universe.

As you are envisioning your hands pulsating the energy representing your intentions, gently rub the candle with the oils you have chosen. You want to make sure you cover the entire candle in whichever direction lines up with your intentions. As you do this, keep your intentions in your mind and heart, feeling the energy and intention filling the candle in your hand. At this point, you can choose to dress the candle if you wish to do so. If you wish to dress the candle, move down to the next section.

Coat the Candle with Magical Herbs

Dressing the candle will help you build up the power of your spell. You can build up extra energy by adding herbs to the candle's oil. This is simple enough—all you will do is select the herbs that will work for you. You will take the herbs, crush them onto a piece of paper, and then roll your anointed herbs into the crumbs. When you do this, you will cause the herbs to stick to the candle. You will not get a perfect coating, but the important part is not to get a perfect layer—what you want to do is make sure that the candle itself is mostly coated.

Choosing the right herbs for you and your purpose can be difficult, but doing so is incredibly beneficial and powerful. You may choose lavender to attract spirits or beauty, or choose patchouli to protect. Frankincense is powerful when it comes to protecting yourself or destroying evil. By and large, many of the herbs that you can use will line up with the anointing oils that will be listed in the Table of Correspondence.

Carving and Engraving

This step will involve you carving symbols into your candle. You will want to choose a symbol that really helps convey the message you are trying to send off into the universe. For example, you may make it a point to use a heart to send your romantic intentions into the world around you, or you may wish to use a dollar sign to attract money. You could also engrave names or astrological signs, or even find some runes that you think will work for you.

When you use this method of anointing your candle, think about what your goal is for the spell you are preparing for. Do you wish to attract a lover? Get money? Protect yourself? Encourage emotional healing or growth? Really consider what you are looking for and imagine that intention swelling within your chest. Close your eyes and try to envision what the intention would look like if it had a physical manifestation. Try to align your symbol with that manifestation, and carve it into your candle.

Remember to be careful and cautious during this step—you do not want to be too rough, or you risk breaking the candle. Not forceful enough, and you risk not having the image engraving properly onto the candle. Of course, this does not have to be perfect, but it can help you focus your intention and really make sure that you are able to send the proper energy out into the universe as it burns. When you are carving the image into the candle, you do not have to necessarily use any specific tool, but it can help to use an athame if you have one. If not, you can use your fingernail to carve it, or even a pen, a tack, a nail, or a toothpick will be good enough to help you carve the intention's manifested symbol into your candle's wax.

As you carve it, continue to imagine your intentions, and you may even choose to recite a chant or affirmation that you feel really encompasses the intention that you are sending out in the first place. With the incantation uttered, if you chose to use one, and your image carved, your candle should be ready to use.

Spray with Holy Water

The last method that is commonly used to consecrate a candle is to create your own holy water and use that to prepare it. Holy water is easy to make—all you need to do is use some water, oil, and salt that you will use to then spray over the candle.

When you are making your holy water, remember that salt is purifying—by adding salt, you create a protective, purifying addition to the water you will be using, and by doing so, you allow the candle to help project your energy into the world. You will start this process by taking a cup of water and mixing three pinches of sea salt into it—try to make sure this is sea salt. Sea salt is much less processed than table salt, making it much better for the use in spells. When you use this sea salt, you allow yourself to tap into the power of the ocean as well as the earth, and you will be applying this to the candle you are going to burn.

With the salt and water mixed together, add a drop or two of an oil of your choice. This oil will really help you get the candle ready. Mix the water and oil into a mister and then stop for a moment, closing your eyes with the mister still in your hands. Really think about the goal of the spell you are about to cast. What do you need to send out into the universe? What is your goal here? Do you wish to make someone come to you? Attract goodness? Expel evil and negativity? Make sure you imagine your intention clearly in your mind, focusing on it, and imagining the intentions flowing straight into the water mister, imbuing the water within it with the same intentions you have.

Now, open your eyes and spray the candle that you are preparing. Repeat your intention here at this point as you spray the candle. You do not need to soak the candle, but a nice quick spray all around will do the job, and at this point, your candle is ready for use.

If you do not have a mister, don't fret! You can use your fingers, much as how you anoint a candle with oil. Instead of spraying, you can simply dip your fingers in the water and let a few drops fall onto the candle, or rub the water along the surface with your fingers, repeating your affirmation and intentions to yourself. This should be enough to prepare your candle.

Now, you can choose to do any or all of these consecration methods. If you are choosing to use all four methods, however, it is recommended that you carve the candle first—if you were to oil it before carving, you run the risk of it slipping out of your hand and potentially hurting yourself on whatever tool you were planning to use on your item in the first place. Of course, you do not want that, so you should make it a point to carve first, then anoint in oil, then the herbs and finally spritz it with the holy spell water if you planned on using all four different methods to consecrate your candle.

No matter what the method you choose, it should feel personal to you, and the entire time that you are going through this process, you should make sure that you are actively allowing your intentions to flow into the candle. You want to ensure that the candle is able to absorb the energy you wish to put into it, so when it burns, the right intentions flow out into the world.

Chapter 4: 7 Simple Steps To Cast Candle Spells

Now, with all of the background information that you could possibly need, it is time to begin casting spells! There are seven steps that will help you achieve this process. All you need to do is go through each and every step as you attempt to create your spell and send your intention into the world. Do not worry too much about the exact process. Wiccan magic is incredibly personal, and the only consistency between people's magic is that you must make sure that you are pushing your intentions out into the world. How that looks to you is entirely personal and up to you.

Remember that your candle is personal and sacred to you. You will prepare each candle for one specific spell unless otherwise noted in the spell that you planned to follow. You will find that you need several different types of spells in your repertoire in order to be well-rounded, but that is okay! This guide will walk you through the general steps that you will go through before introducing you to several spells that you may find to be useful to you.

Choose Your Supplies

Perhaps the most fundamental step to this process is choosing out your supplies. These are going to be specific to you most of the time. The one consistency is adding in a candle. Nevertheless, even the kind of candle that you choose will vary based on the purpose you are attempting to create. Make sure that the candle will work for you. While a glass pillar candle may be beautiful and contain the mess, for example it will not do you any favors if you needed to carve a rune or other message into its surface, as you cannot possibly do so through the glass. If you want to use oil and herbs, you may choose a candle that is not a tealight one—noting that the tealight candle is far too small to be effective.

You must also note that your candle's scent, if applicable, size, and general shape will be appropriate. You do not want a big candle to burn if your spell is supposed to be short. For example you want to make the candle thinner so it can burn quicker and easier.

Beyond the candles, you need to make sure you identify which herbs and oils you will use for anointing if you choose to use them. You will need a candleholder for your candle, especially if it is a taper candle that is too narrow to effectively stand on its own. Beyond that, you will want to make sure you gather any items for your altar. You may choose to have charms, symbols, or talismans present on your altar while you perform your candle magic.

Prepare Your Workspace

The next step will be to prepare your workspace. You want to ensure that you have the right ambiance, set up your altar just right, and ensure that everything is exactly as it should be. Remember that you are working with fire, so you want to make sure you are somewhere that is not a fire risk. Try setting up somewhere without curtains or a tablecloth, especially if you have children that may run by and upset everything. You want to ensure that the area is as fireproof as possible. You may even choose to place your candle into a fireproof dish, such as a cauldron or cast-iron pot in order to prevent any tips from causing problems for you. In fact, you may instead opt to gently ban all children and pets from your room when you are in the process of performing the spell in the first place. By removing them altogether, you can ensure that there are no burnt paws or tiny fingers that may have been a bit too curious and got a bit too close to where they should not have been.

This is also a good time to make sure that you prepare yourself as well. Be mindful of the clothing and way that you wear your hair as you prepare your spell. If you have long hair, you may want to consider tying it into a bun or placing it within a hat or a high-sitting ponytail to keep it out of harm's way. You will want to make sure that you are not wearing any clothing with long sleeves that drape or flow—as nice as you may look wearing that beautiful gown with the flowing sleeves. Those sleeves could very easily accidentally dip into the flame of the candle and ruin the entire process.

With the safety out of the way, it is time to start considering the method through which you will set up your workplace. You can change this up, making it personal to you, but as a general rule, the candle is usually right in the middle of the altar for candle spells, with perhaps a few additional aspects included. You may have salt, herbs, seashells, crystals, or other items present that would then impact the spell or potentially even bolster the effect of the intentions you have been presenting to the universe altogether.

As a general rule, you should make sure you gather all of your ingredients beforehand, so make sure you have everything with you. If you are right-handed, perhaps you will keep your tools to the right of your altar, lining up your athame if you have one, your crystals, and anything else you may find that you need. On the left, you may decide to keep your Book of Shadows and any resources that will help guide you through the spell that you were planning to utilize. By setting up, so you have everything present for you all at one time, you will avoid running into trouble if you, for example, decided that you no longer have one of the tools you needed on hand. It may also help to keep your water, wine, tea, or anything else that you may decide to drink next to you, so you do not have to stop your spell to quench your thirst if push comes to shove.

As you prepare, just remember one thing: This altar is for you. You do not need to worry about offerings for a Deity unless you planned on using one in your spell. It should be set up in the best way that works for you with no regard to respecting others or looking pretty. It is meant to be functional, and if you can use it, then it is.

Carving And Dressing

This step is all about preparing your candle for use in your spell. This can happen in several different ways, as you learned about—for this example, we will go through carving and dressing, but the carving is entirely optional.

When you chose to carve your candle, remember that you should make sure that the image that you carve into your candle should be useful to the spell, embodying the intention that you are hoping to portray into the world. This means that you may choose to carve a dollar sign for money or a heart for a love spell. Instead, you may write names or otherwise draw something. This does not have to be fancy or intricate—you can literally write a word or name of whatever you hope to receive from the universe into your candle.

Keep in mind, however, that you should always have several back-up candles available. Snapping candles, especially in the early days, is quite common, and if you snap your last candle, you are going to have to stop this process altogether. However, remember, you can simply skip the carving step altogether if you prefer!

When you are dressing your candle, you are rubbing it with oil and then rolling it into dried herbs. This process will help you power the candle, especially if you can murmur your intentions as you apply the oil. If you add the herbs to this process as well, they can help supplement the power, creating a spell that you know will be effective and beneficial to you and help you send out the proper intentions into the world.

If you are short on oil, you can always use olive oil—which is commonly found in kitchens. While many people prefer to use essential oils that will line up with their intentions, you can always choose to use a neutral oil such as olive oil or vegetable oil—you simply need to add the oil to the surface of the candle. Again, remember to be mindful of the direction of the anointment, but ultimately, the direction you push the oil should be personal to you. After all, this entire process is all about doing what works best for you, allowing you to project your intentions to the universe in the most effective manner possible. In doing so, you should see the best result.

With your candle oiled, it is time to add ground herbs, if you have chosen to do so. Of course, this is also dependent upon the spell that you are casting and your own intention, but if you choose to add an herb, you likely have some within your kitchen right now that could be helpful—all that matters is that the herbs are finely crushed and you can roll them onto your candle.

With your candle prepared, set it onto your candleholder and go clean up—no one wants to complete a spell involving fire with oily, slippery hands!

Light The Candle

When you are cleaned up, it is time to light the candle. This is quite simple, but the process can be is intimate and intricate as you would like. Lighters and matches are just fine for this, or you can choose to use a piece of incense that is on fire, or use the light from another candle to light yours. Ultimately, so long as your candle ends up lit, you are good. After all, your spell won't really work if you can't get the candlelit in the first place.

As you light your candle, make sure that you take a moment to consider the intentions that you are hoping to instill within your candle. Do you want someone else to be attracted to you? Imagine the other person and make it a point to focus on him or her for a moment as you hold the flame before using it to ignite the candle. Focus your intention, allowing it to flow into your lighter or match before using it to burn the candle as well.

As the flame takes, you can then allow your intention to flow straight into the candle as well. It should be burning strongly, fortified by the oil, herbs, carving, and your intention as it influences the energy of the universe.

Focus On Intention

This next step is all about sending your intention out into the universe as the candle is burning for you. You can meditate, inwardly focusing on your intention in a state of mindfulness. You can daydream and visualize your intention coming to fruition. All that matters is that you are actively focusing on your intention and sending it out into the universe. Here, we can go over several different options for how to go about this process.

Meditation

When you are meditating, you are focusing inwardly. You want to stop and focus on you yourself. Take a deep breath in, feeling the air enter your lungs, and then breathe out. As you breathe out, imagine that your intention, which is filling your entire body, is being exerted outward into the world. You want to allow this energy to flow outwards, emanating from each and every part of your body as the candle flickers. Watch the flame and imagine your own intentions flickering like the flame as you continue to breathe deeply to control yourself. Allow yourself to relax further, and imagine your intention emanating further and further away from you with each and every breath. You will do this as you breathe, waiting for the candle to burn.

Visualization

When you are using visualization instead of meditating, you are focusing more on imagining how you feel when you receive whatever you were attempting to receive. Rather than feeling your intentions flow outwards around you, you are envisioning yourself as the universe answers your prayers and gives you exactly what you were looking to obtain. In doing so, you attract that positive energy back toward you. When you do this, then you can really encourage the universe to answer your prayers for you. As you visualize, you want to focus on the entire process and how it feels—you want to welcome the arrival of your desires, imagining feeling it, smelling it, responding to it, and otherwise interacting with it. If your desire is a specific person to become attracted to you, for example, you would imagine that person coming to you affectionately, coming to give you a kiss. You would imagine the smell of the other person, the feel of their hand brushing along your face, and maybe even the sound of their voice declaring that they love you. You would then envision how you would feel and respond to this situation, all while listening to the sound of the candle flickering while you projected those visualizations to the candle as it burns.

Chanting

As you are chanting, you will be voicing your intentions outward for the universe to hear. This can be anything that you feel really helps you project the intention out. Many people prefer to use some sort of rhyming technique, believing it easier to fall into a rhythmic chant, which can then aid in the relaxation and meditation stage of this process. Others may simply allow for their vocalization of whatever comes to mind at that moment, creating a constant stream of thought while they imagine their intentions arriving to them. There is no real rule here—all that matters is that you are able to project your will into the universe for it to hear and respond to. After all, even your voice consists of vibrations, so just by speaking, you are altering the state of the universe at will.

Journaling

Some people may decide to journal rather than attempting to go through the chanting process. If you are doing this, you can do one of two things—you may try writing onto a piece of paper that you can burn into the candle, or you can leave your notes in your Book of Shadows—ultimately, the choice is yours for what you would like to do. If you feel like you will put out more energy by voicing your intentions out loud, that is fine, but if you think that burning a physical manifestation of your intention will help, that works too! What is important about this stage is that you are doing something that comes naturally to you, and you are doing so in a way that focuses your energy on several different layers, all building up to influence the universe around you.

You should do this process as long as it feels comfortable to you. Remember, this is a very personal process, and there is no right or wrong way to cast your spell into the world around you. If you think that you are done after five minutes, that is fine. If you feel comfortable going until it burns out, that is fine as well. Go with your intuition here—that intuition is the God and Goddess guiding you through the world and imploring you to listen to their guidance. They are there with you, especially as you are casting your spell if you are willing to open your mind and your heart and listen for them. Let their Divine Judgment guide you as you make your decision on when to end your spell.

Flame Extinction

As you feel your spell wrap to a close, feeling like you have gotten out your message loud and clear, you can choose how to end the spell. This comes as a point of contention for some people—they feel like you must absolutely leave your candle to burn itself out. They feel like if you were to blow out your candle, you have killed the energy that you have put out, ruining your intention, and stopping it from coming back to you. Others, however, feel like the breath is a powerful way to use your own energy. You are harnessing the element of air when you blow on something, and if anything, breathing out and blowing out your candle would be sending your intention into the air itself rather than killing your intention altogether.

Again, this is a very personal decision that you will have to make for yourself. You need to decide on your own whether you feel like blowing out your candle is destroying your intention or whether it is merely bolstering its energy, making it a proper way to bring an end to your spell if you choose to do so. Do not be afraid to blow out your candle, but at the same time, do not be afraid to let it burn down itself either.

Some spells will require you to burn the candle down to its own extinction, and that is okay. You should follow this process—especially if it is a magic that involves the banishment of an energy or purification. Those spells, when you allow them to burn themselves down, maybe more thorough, but at the end of the day, there are still exceptions to this process.

If you must leave your home or the room, it is important to blow out the candle—you do not ever want to leave a candle unattended. Too much can happen if you leave it unattended—a child could knock it over, or a gust of wind or a bump to the table it is sitting on could happen, causing the candle to fall. While you may really want to purify your home or banish all evil from a room, the right way to do is not by burning your home down inadvertently due to leaving the candle unattended. Ultimately, if you must interrupt the spell, that is better than leaving the candle burning unattended.

Remember, fire itself is so incredibly powerful—leaving it to its own devices without someone to tame it is a risk that no one should take, no matter what. A half-finished spell is better than risking a fire that could devastate your family of a family nearby.

Nevertheless, extinguishing the flame does bring your process to a close. When you blow out the flame, you are ending the flow of magic and energy out into the universe. All that is left now is the proper disposal of any remnants of the spell that you have finished.

Disposing Of Remnants

The final step, disposing of the remnants of the spell, is incredibly personal. Everyone has a different opinion on it so you will have to choose what works best for you. Again, follow your intuition. Ultimately, that is going to be the best guide for you to go through the process and determine what works best for you. Do not worry about what other people are doing with their remnants—choose the solution that resonates with you.

Some people prefer to throw their remnants into the garbage—this is a valid solution! You can absolutely choose to dump out your remnants and move forward with your day without a second thought. This may be one of the most efficient methods in terms of how much time you have available to you. However, it is also one of the most impersonal. For some, this is seen as disrespectful to your spell, the intention, and the universe.

Others prefer to burn their remnants in a fire. This can be another valid decision, especially in the winter, if you have a fireplace and will have a fire lit anyway. However, if you have to go out of your way to start a fire, you are effectively just making extra work for yourself in disposing of the remains.

Another method of disposing of your remnants is through choosing to bury their remnants. This can be a great way to manage them, but you must make sure that everything is biodegradable, and you should try to avoid burying anything near the water. Also, burying salts, in particular, can cause the area to become barren and infertile.

Some people choose to let their ashes go into the wind, and others choose to dump the remains into the water. As you can see, people will usually choose an element that really resonates with them and will use those methods to dispose of the remains, but you should try to avoid dumping many remnants into the water unless you are dumping it into a toilet, where the water will be filtered and processed, so it does not impact wildlife.

One last option that people sometimes use is keeping the remnants for use later, especially if you choose to reverse the spell at any given point—however, if you wish to hold onto these, you will want to clearly label them. You may try writing down the summary of the spell, the intention, and how it was done, as well as when and where, onto a piece of paper and include that with the remnants for future reference.

That's really all there is to it—most spells that you perform, especially with your candles. When you are going through these spells, you can sum them up into the above seven steps.

Chapter 5: Candle Spells To Foster Love And Relationships

Passion fades in relationships—even the healthiest of marriages will have periods where passion and desire run low. Of course, this can be to one partner's chagrin or annoyance, but it is normal. Passions ebb and flow, but that does not necessarily mean that the relationship itself is struggling or damaged—when your relationships see the levels of desire fade away, it simply means that you or your partner is simply not as interested in physical intimacy as usual. This will usually pass, and you will find that you rediscover your spark at some point. Nevertheless, when you feel like you would rather not wait for that passion to return, you can use these spells to build it up quicker than ever before. In fact, you may be able to see the end results almost immediately, suddenly triggering a change within your relationship.

These will bring love back into your life, triggering feelings of passion, stronger than ever before. With that passion and intimacy rekindled, your relationship will feel stronger than ever. This magic is not necessarily evil or dark—it is all about returning to your roots, rediscovering old feelings rather than forcing someone else into allowing you to have your way with them. This is entirely dependent upon feelings that already exist in the other person, and without them, these spells may as well be useless. They will not do anything without the right feelings, or at least the right seeds of feelings within the other person.

When you use these spells, burning your candle for the other person, you are going to see your relationships transform quickly. Keep in mind that this will trigger all sorts of new sexual desires—that is one of the feelings that helps encourage and foster romantic passion. When you go through these spells, you are not necessarily hurting anyone, but you will be instilling an urge of sexual energy within yourself and your partner—this is not necessarily harmful, but you and your partner will be drawn together far more than usual.

When this happens, make sure you are discreet, but enjoy the newfound passion that you have developed. You will find your confidence boosted up quickly and effectively as your partner suddenly longs for you left and right, making you feel far more attractive than you did before. That sudden boost in confidence could be everything that you needed in the bedroom, allowing you both to up the ante a bit and get creative and intimate.

Awakened Desire Spell

This spell is perfect for attracting someone else to you—it can make the person that you love fall in love even deeper with you, working by using your own desires to help awaken the desire within the heart of another. It is the most effective when the other person loves you, as what you will be doing is unlocking that tiny speck of desire for you, expanding, and growing it much like how a seed develops from a sprout into a mighty tree.

This is not manipulative—you are taking control of feelings that are already there and then expanding upon them, swaying them, and opening them up. You are opening their mind to the possibility, and by doing so, you are able to ensure that they are feeling their truest feelings that are not artificial— all you did was set them free to exist as they desired to do so. If the other person feels love for you after this spell, it was because the love for you was already there, blocked behind some sort of obstacle or reservation.

To complete this spell, you will need a handful of items. Gather up three pieces of parchment—two are small, and one is large. Make sure that you also have a wooden pencil—specifically wooden. Bring one pink candle, sandalwood oil, and cinnamon incense. You will also need a box of wooden matches, a red ribbon, and three gems—a rose quartz, a jade, and an emerald.

Now, you are going to begin by casting a circle.

When you wish to cast your circle, imagine the boundaries of your circle surrounding you. Slowly and meticulously, imagine the circle filling with energy and surrounding you with light—this circle will keep you protected and allow you to process your spell without interruption from negative energy. Some people prefer to go through this process by setting up the circle around them in a physical manner. You may choose to draw it with chalk, set up candles or rocks, or even salt to mark where your circle's boundaries are. As the God and Goddess to join you and help you energize your circle.

With the circle around you, it is time to begin the spell. Anoint a pink candle with sandalwood oil and then light the cinnamon incense, along with the candle. As you do this, you are able to go through the process of encouraging the other person to unlock the love hiding within their hearts for you.

At this point, take your two pieces of paper and a pencil. Sit down and slowly and neatly write your name onto one piece of paper. Make sure you include your entire name—first, middle, and last. Then, take the second paper and repeat this process for the other person that you wish would fall in love with you. With both names written carefully and neatly, you should draw a heart around each name with the pencil.

Then, take the candle into your dominant hand and drop wax down onto the hearts over the names. As the wax drips down upon your hand, make sure that you focus on the world around you, sending your wish out for it to hear. Call to the universe, imploring it to send your feelings of love to your loved one, allowing the energy to help unblock his or her heart. Follow your intuition as you do this—

you will know when to stop dripping the wax and building the energy within yourself.

Now, turn to the larger piece of parchment and write down your desires. Make sure you take your time, elaborating exactly what you wish for. If you wish for your loved one to unlock his heart, for example, note that down. If you wish that your loved one returned your feelings, include that as well. This does not necessarily need to follow a specific sentence structure or rhyme or anything, but it should feel natural and right to you. Do this in any way that works well for you, allowing yourself to write down your feelings and intentions. Really allow your feelings of love and desire to flow through the pencil, using the wood as a conduit for your energy.

With the feelings, all recorded and written down on the parchment, place the smaller pieces with the names atop it and wrap them together. Take your piece of ribbon and tie the bundle closed, making three knots. Then, you will want to place all three stones, the quartz, jade, and emerald atop the package that you made. This will charge the paper with the love attraction that the crystals bring with them. Allow this package to sit atop your altar as your candle continues to burn.

At this point, sit and meditate upon your intentions as you wait for the candle to burn out. When it has gone out on its own, you should take your package, without the crystals, and find a private hiding place for it. You do not want this to be found by someone else.

Eternal Love Spell

This spell will help you grow the love between yourself and your partner. There is already love lingering between the two of you, and you are simply encouraging it to continue growing, making sure that it never ends.

This spell, in particular, should be started on a Friday and will take seven days. In particular, try to begin this process on the Friday during the next Waxing Moon, allowing you to then utilize the magic of the Moon's energy as well as the magic from your candles.

For this spell, you will need either a white or gold candle to represent a man, and a black or silver candle to represent a woman—if there are two men or two women in the relationship, adjust accordingly. All you would do is use two gold or two silver candles instead of one of each. Then, you need a green candle to bring attraction, a tool to carve the candles, and a piece of green cloth.

Start this spell by casting your circle and calling the quarters—in this instance; you are asking for the elements to join you as you place water to the west of the circle, fire to the south, air to the east, and earth to the north. With the circle cast, it is time to start.

With the carving tool you have chosen, mark the candles with something personal for each person—may be an astrological sign. Then, make seven equal marks across the green candle horizontally. These will be your guide for how long to allow the candle to burn. Put the male candle on the right side of the altar and then the female candle to the left, roughly a foot apart from each other, and then put the green candle between them, but pushed back slightly on your altar in order to form a triangle.

Now, focus on your partner—really imagine their face in your mind and your feelings for them flowing around you. Light your candle first, followed by the candle for the other person, and then light the green one last. You will now quietly meditate about the process, encouraging the love between your partner and you to grow and last forever. As you do this, imagine how the two of you feel together until the green candle has melted down to the first notch you have made. Now, extinguish your candle, followed by the candle for your partner, and then lastly, the green candle.

On day two, you will repeat the same process, but this time, you will position the candles slightly closer together. You will then light them in the same order, following the same steps. Each day, you will move the candles slightly closer together until they are finally touching on day seven. On this day, you should allow all three candles to burn themselves out. Then, wrap up the wax and store it somewhere safe.

Lunar Lust Spell

What is a solid relationship without a little lust between partners? However, in relationships, that passion can ebb and flow regularly—you may find that it is difficult to relate to your partner or really get intimate sometimes, especially if the relationship is long-term and there are other outside stressors. Perhaps you and your partner have young children, for example. Early parenthood is not really thought of as being very highly full of sex. Nevertheless, with a bit of help from a candle, you can set up some Lunar Lust between you and your partner, hopefully sparking a bit of romance between you with little effort.

This spell will require you to gather a single red candle, musk oil, rose incense, a picture of your loved one, and a bowl that will withstand fire. Preferably, you will wait until the Waxing Moon for this spell, but if you absolutely cannot wait, you can try at other points in time too.

First, cast your circle and use your chosen method to consecrate your candle. Then, anoint the candle with your musk oil before lighting the candle. Then, you must light your rose incense and place your loved one's photo in front of the candle.

With the candlelit, it is time to chant:

"Eros, the presiding God of Lust and Passion,

Bolster [Loved one's name]'s feeling of euphoric lust in a hurried fashion.

Awaken within [Loved one's name] a need for physical affection,

As well as [his/her] sexual attraction

Cause [Loved one's name] to lust and long for me,

And I shall respectfully accept that plea

So, mote it be

So, mote it be."

Then, pick up the candle in your dominant hand and allow it to spill some wax onto the picture. When you do this, implore the Moon to hear your plea, and send your intentions out to Eros, asking both to kindly aid you in your endeavors. You want them to hear you, projecting your intentions out as much as you can as you watch the candle burn. Try to focus your energy, encouraging it to burn and smolder like the candle in your hand. Imagine that your energy is being released with each and every flicker of the flame.

When you have done so, place the candle back on the holder and allow the candle to burn out. When it is done, hide the photograph underneath your bed until you no longer need it—whether your relationship ends or you find that the relationship has developed the passion that it used to have. When you no longer have a need for it, return it to the great Earth that helped you—you could burn it and let the ashes go free or bury it if it is biodegradable.

Burning Desire Spell

The next spell you will do is to encourage a desire for you, exciting lust, and building the desire to seek you out. You are essentially going to tap into the thoughts of the other person and bring forth those that desire you. It will push away negative thoughts that may be preventing your partner or the object of your desire from seeing you as a viable partner. With the negative thoughts out of the way, you should be free to move forward with the relationship.

For this spell, you will need a handful of objects—you will want to gather a red candle, one tablespoon of damiana, one tablespoon of galangal, two tablespoons of cayenne pepper, one tablespoon of coriander, orange oil, and lastly, a knife and mortar.

With your ingredients gathered, you are ready to trigger lust to reappear in your relationship, allowing for passion to be reborn with ease.

Begin first by crushing the herbs into a fine powder and set it aside. Then, you will need to carve the name of yourself and your loved one into the candle. Be careful during this—you may want to use a nail or something else small in order to carve these in, especially if the candle is particularly thin. Remember to start with a new candle if your breaks under the force of writing the names.

With the names written, it is time to anoint your candle. Start with the orange oil at the top, beginning at the wick, and slowly make your way down the body of the candle until you reach the bottom. As you do this, clear your mind from negativity and instead allow yourself to be filled with feelings of love and passion for your partner, or whoever you are casting the spell upon.

With the candle anointed, roll the candle in the powder from the herbs, coating it as much as possible, but this does not have to be perfect. As long as at least some of the herbs stick, you should be fine. As you get the powder onto the candle, start thinking about the individual once more. Really imagine them and allow yourself first to be filled with a burning desire for them.

Place the candle on the altar and then light it as it sits in its holder and repeat the following chant at least 7 times:

"Kalimesto Paridako Helistati [lover's name here]
Kalimesto Paraidako Helistati
Stabulo Balika Ro [your name here]
Hambuta Salika Te"

Then, you should allow your candle to burn for an hour as you sit and meditate on your own feelings for the other person, attempting to project them into the world around you as clearly as you possibly can. After the hour is up, blow out the candle.

You will then repeat this process for six more days, with you allowing the candle to burn until it has completed itself on the seventh day. After doing so, you should find that the spell is beginning to work.

Voodoo Attraction Spell

This last love spell is meant to attract your loved one to you, keeping your passion burning for each other, or helping you rekindle that attraction if you have found that it has faded away somewhat. Through this spell, you will see differences almost immediately—by reenergizing the passion in your relationship; you should start to see that you and your partner begin to look at each other lovingly again. Before we begin, there is a quick disclaimer—this particular spell should be performed somewhere private, preferably behind a locked and closed door. At the end of the ritual, you will be masturbating as a part of the process, and that should always be done somewhere discreetly to avoid any potential interruptions or scarring anyone else for life if they were to suddenly stumble upon you.

This is a voodoo spell—this means that it is harnessing the energy of the world to encourage the changes that are desired. In particular, the older, primal energies are the ones that are often influenced the most. When you use this spell, then, you are interacting with lust, one of the most basic feelings that humans have, meant to drive us to reproduce and meet our biological imperative. It is a powerful tool, and you will be able to use it effectively and easily.

When you utilize this, you should see your relationship improve almost immediately. Keep in mind that as you use this, you should not be alarmed if you see a change immediately—it does lead to higher lusting after your partner.

To complete this spell, you will need cinnamon incense, a red candle, red ink (dove's blood ink, preferably), a piece of paper, a photo of the individual that you are seeking to target, ground caraway seeds, ground dill, cinnamon, brown sugar, yarn, and you will call upon Dumballah and Ayida, his wife.

Start by lighting your incense, and then light the candle next to it. Then, mix up the sugar with the cinnamon, dill, and caraway. You want it to be well-blended. With the paper in front of you, write your partner's name upon the paper and then atop their name, write your own, literally writing over their own name, so they overlap. With your names there, sprinkle the herbs and sugar atop it all.

At this point, you should start focusing your intentions, really envisioning exactly what you were hoping to achieve, and then allow yourself to call upon Dumballah and Ayida. Ask for their help as you continue to sprinkle the sugar and herbs. When the mixture is entirely poured out, pick up the picture and place it atop the sugar and herbs.

Now, turn off the lights, leaving only the candlelight for you to see by. Take this time to masturbate as you imagine your partner and ensure that you achieve orgasm. Imagine that your own sexual energy is going out into the universe toward the individual that you are targeting with your own release. As you do so, think about your partner, imagining everything that you wish to do to him or her when the spell is complete as you go through the process. Make sure that you think of your partner or the target of this spell the entire time. When you finish up with yourself, make sure that you place some of your own bodily fluids onto the photo to really seal everything up and ensure that nothing will be spilling out. After all, no one wants spices all over their floor.

Wrap up everything in the paper and tie it shut while you wait for the candle to burn out, reflecting upon the process and imagining the end results of the spell. You really want to send your intentions out into the universe, allowing the candle to send your energy toward the target of your desire. Once the candle finally does go out, take the package, and hide it somewhere in your room, typically as close to the bed as possible. If you can, place it underneath your mattress, near your head. When you no longer need this, you should return it to the Earth, burying it or burning it and scattering the ashes.

Chapter 6: Spells To Attract Money And Success

Do you have enough money in your life? How about success? Money and success are two things that you can never have too much of in your life. After all, despite the fact that you cannot buy happiness itself, you can have the money to pay for everything you need in order to require you to work less so you have more time to pursue the things that make you happy. Effectively then, money may not buy happiness, but it certainly can buy the time that you will need to pursue that happiness once and for all.

When you use these spells, you will be focusing on attracting everything in life that you need—good things do not just appear randomly or happen due to good or bad luck. Rather, they are attracted. If you think optimistically, you are more likely to achieve success than someone who is thinking pessimistically. If you think that your relationship will be effective, you will most likely work through your problems whereas if you feel like your relationship is a waste of time, you may not bother to fix a problem and instead break up or end the relationship rather than ever trying in the first place.

Of course, this principle can lean toward money too. If you feel like you will be successful, inviting money and wealth into your life, you may find that you are more likely to find that money and success than if you feel like you will never be able to provide for yourself or your family. This means, then, that if you want to be successful and effective in life, you need to figure out how to repel the mental and spiritual blockages that may be causing you problems and welcome the positive energy that will act as a magnet for the money and success you may need.

Keep in mind that while you may be having a money problem at the moment, it may not be because you are bad with money or because you are unlucky— instead, it could directly be linked to your own emotional state. You may be envious of those around you, and that envy can cause people to do things that may not be the smartest decision. You may be indecisive, and that causes you to miss opportunities. You may be a major procrastinator, meaning you are never doing the work to get the money that you are seeking in the first place.

Keep in mind that these spells will not make money magically line your pockets, or even make you suddenly find the money on the side of the road. Instead, these spells will work to clear your mind and send out positive intentions and energy into the world, encouraging you to behave in ways that are conducive to earning and receiving money. With your mind cleared, and you find yourself free of indecisiveness, anxiety, fear, guilt, or anything else that is currently holding you back, you may find that you actually can achieve receiving money after all. You may land yourself a better job, using the energy that the world and the universe sent back to you to make yourself more desirable. You may use the energy to get that raise that you were interviewing for or to encourage yourself to develop a relationship with someone who is able to help you get a job that will pay you what you need. You may even get lucky and win the lottery or something else that will make the money just suddenly fall into your lap, but that is not the norm—it may happen for some, but do not come to expect that reaction.

As you go through these spells, you will learn how to form the mindset that will help you become spiritually and emotionally wealthy, and as that happens, the finances will follow suit almost effortlessly, creating the money that you need to solve your problems altogether.

7-Day Wealth And Abundance Spell

This first spell that you are going to cast is simple and easy—all you will need is a green candle, a paper and pen, and a holder for the candle, so it does not cause any damage. This spell will involve you visualizing the success that you so strongly desire. You will be searching within yourself, visualizing that you can achieve your goals. As you visualize this ending, you are constantly building intention and sending out energy. The candle will help you focus that intention, allowing you to really harness the energy within yourself and send it out appropriately.

As this happens, you will, of course, have room within yourself opened up, which you can then use to ensure that you find what you were looking for all along. You may be able to ask the world around you to provide you with peace of mind, for example, and that intention will return, with that intention, then bringing with it the ability for you to find the wealth that you desired for so long.

To begin this spell, you must begin by drawing on your paper. Start by drawing a symbol for your local currency. If you live in the United States, you would draw the dollar sign, but for those of you out of the country, you can draw the sign of the pounds, the euro, or even the yen, depending on the currency that you will be using. This drawing should be somewhat large and made neatly. With the sign drawn on the paper, you should then decorate the dollar sign that you have drawn, allowing yourself to doodle whatever you would like onto it. Make this with any signs that are personal to you—perhaps you may include a representation of yourself, of the God and Goddess, who you trust implicitly, or anything else.

As you draw on your paper, focus your breathing. Make sure that you follow the strokes of your pen with your eyes as you take deep breaths—you should take each inhale and exhale for at least four, but preferably five seconds at a time. When you do this, you help your body enter a state of meditation and focus. With a clearer mind, sending out your intentions becomes easier than ever. When you feel relaxed, and your money symbol is finished, close your eyes, and visualize the amount of money you need for a moment—this should be an amount that is not insane to ask for and expect. It could be something small, such as enough to pay for a single bill or perhaps to make sure you have food for the week. With that number in your mind's eye, visualizing it in your bank account as you do so, write down the number on the paper.

Place the paper down on the altar and then set the candle holder with the candle atop the paper. At this point, you could anoint the green candle if you chose to do so, inviting prosperity or luck and carving money signs into it. You can, of course, choose to skip doing this if you wish. Light the candle in the candle holder.

Now, you will begin that breathing exercise once more. With deep breaths in and out, imagine the money arriving to you in some way. For fifteen minutes as the candle burns, you should focus on all of the ways that the money could arrive. Perhaps you could get a sudden bonus at work, or suddenly get a promotion because of a change in attitude.

Maybe you happened to find the money in a pair of pants that you had thought were lost. Maybe you found the money on the ground while walking your dog. Maybe someone left you a tip somewhere.

If you are unsure about how the money could possibly arrive for you, that is okay too. Instead of worrying about it, clear your mind and relax, focusing instead entirely on your breathing. The money will come to your mind eventually in some fashion—you may realize that you actually do have that kind of money somewhere, or you may decide that you can sell something you own that you never leave, which conveniently, would be worth about what you needed anyway.

Continue your meditations as your candle continues to burn. You should watch the candle, observing how the wax drips down the candlestick and onto the paper beneath it. If you find that it is not dripping down onto the paper below, you can instead carefully tilt the stick to allow some of the wax to dropdown. Be careful when doing this—you do not want to burn yourself on the flame or on the hot wax.

When the candle has spilled the wax onto the paper, you can then blow out the candle. You will repeat this for seven days, using the same candle for every iteration of the spell.

Ocean Wealth Attraction Spell

This next spell is designed to focus on the power of salt, using it to absorb all of the negativity that may be holding you down, instead inviting positive vibes into your home. This powerful ritual utilizes all four elements at the same time—drawing from earth, air, fire, and water to create powerful intentions and energies that will be allowed to flow out into the universe, hopefully returning to you the desired result.

This spell is best done during the Full or Waxing Moon, somewhere that you are free to act without interruption. However, it will still be effective, even if it is not one of those Moons. To represent earth, you will use sea salt. To represent water, you will use seashells. To represent fire, you will use candles, and to represent air, you will use any type of incense that you may have on hand at that point in time. Any scent will be fine.

Start by preparing your altar—place a dish or a candleholder in the center of the altar. Now, it is time to anoint your candles. You will need one white candle as well as two green ones to represent the prosperity that you are attempting to absorb and attract. Use an oil such as peppermint or cinnamon, which is meant to invite wealth. You can also choose to carve into your candle for extra effect at this stage.

With the candles prepared, you can place all three onto the dish or candleholder. Then, make it a point to light your incense sticks as well. At this point, add seashells all around the base of the candles, decorating them however you wish. This can involve a single seashell that you love, or it could be a pile of shells—any number is just fine. Go with your own gut decision and choose, however many shells as you see fit.

Next, you will take a handful of your sea salt. If you do not have sea salt, try using Epsom salt, or in a pinch, you can use table salt, but it usually is not quite as potent or powerful since it has been so processed. With the handful of salt, create a circle around the seashells and the candles—everything should be within the circle. You want your candles and shells to be entirely protected by the purifying measures of the salt, so they are free to welcome in the good energy that they are seeking.

With the salt surrounding them, it is time to light the candles. With a match or lighter, light each of the three candles, spending the time to really visualize and reflect on the energy that will draw the money toward you. You want to keep in mind exactly what you are hoping to receive or achieve at this point, allowing yourself to see the number in your bank account, or to see the end result of why you need the money in the first place. How much do you need? Why do you need the money? Imagine these things as you go through the rest of this spell.

With all three candles lit, then it is time to really visualize and focus on what you have set out to achieve. If you have sought out money, you will focus on that. If you have sought out success, you may choose to focus on that. If you are looking to get satisfaction, you will focus on that. As you go through this stage, you should focus on these desires and visualizations, envisioning that you are actively already achieving them. How would you feel if you were successful? If you got that job application?

With another handful of sea salt, allow it to sprinkle onto the seashells while you say:

"Many thanks, the Elements of the Universe,
For communing with me, providing for me, and
Bringing me these wondrous gifts of Life.
My life is rich with money and wealth.
I am succeeding in everything I attempt, and I
walk in prosperity
In complete peace and in a perfect manner as it is.
So, mote it be."

Now, allow the candles to burn without interruption. When they finish burning, gather up the wax and salt and flush them down the toilet to allow water to take them away, or allow a river or stream to take the remains. If you cannot do so, then throwing them away will have to suffice.

Make sure you keep the seashells—preferably in an area that you will see regularly, using them as a reminder that money will be coming soon.

Prosperity Spell

This spell is an appeal to St. Expeditus, the commander of a legion in Rome that once defended the Empire from invasion. He was then made a martyr, developing quite a cult during the 18th century, where he was quickly deemed to be the patron saint of both merchants and navigators, becoming a sort of protector of those who are young, sick, and in need of help with their money, workplace, or family problems, and he is even believed to oversee court cases.

When you are using this spell, it is going to be the most effective if you begin on a Sunday morning. All you will need to do is ask to receive. After all, if you never ask, can you really be upset or disappointed when you do not receive? You only need four items during this particular spell—you will want to bring coarse salt, such as sea salt or Epsom salt, a prayer card or image of St. Expeditus, a single white candle, and your chalice, though any cup will do if you do not yet have one.

Start by filling up the cup or chalice with the salt, placing the cup onto your altar. Remember, salt is purifying and also projects out strong positive energies, so by using this, you are neutralizing negativity and magnifying your positive hopes. Take the picture of St. Expeditus and place it into the cup, making sure that at least some of the picture is deep enough that it touches the salt.

Now, choose whether or not you want to consecrate your candle—you may choose to anoint it with oil and symbol that will attract money to you, or you may choose to skip this step altogether, though really, carving a few money symbols would only take a moment and can only help! With the candle prepared, or with this step skipped if you so prefer, you then can light the candle, forming your intention as you do so.

Then, you are going to focus on the image of the saint within the cup, really focusing on your intention. Remain here for a moment, taking a deep breath before moving on. When it is time to continue, you will then begin the following prayer to him:

"Dear Saint Expeditus,
Divine defender of the anguished,
You are the Saint of just and urgent causes.
I shut my eyes,
I give myself to you and trust you.
Please help me, sovereign saint,
Lend me your hand so I can rise up.
So that I can resolve my debts.
Over me Money will rain,
So, I will lack nothing.
Because you have aided me,
I will invoke your Holy Name,
Speaking your thanks and praising your
Sacred Flame.
Amen."

Upon finishing the prayer, you can now allow the candle to finish burning. Make sure that you stay in the room the entire time, focusing on the intention to make money come to you, helping you to alleviate your financial troubles once and for all. When you do this, imagine this, you are projecting your energy to St. Expeditus and to the universe, creating an opening for the universe to send the money to you.

When the candle burns out all the way, it is time to then take the candle out of the chalice and place it into your wallet, taking a small pinch of salt with you, placing that in your wallet as well. The rest of the remains of the spell are free to be thrown away or otherwise disposed of however you see fit.

This spell is meant to tap into the universe, welcoming the arrival of the money it may choose to provide you. If you get this money, you will find that you are better off, all because you asked and you received. If you do not receive the money, you are no worse off than you were before, so you still have lost nothing—just have faith, reflect on what may have gone wrong, and try this spell again in the future.

9-Days Money Attraction Spell

This is the last of the money attraction spells—it is just as simple as the others that have been done thus far. In this spell, you are attempting to attract money to you in several ways. You are going to be using a spell inspired by the Catholic novena—a specific kind of ritual that is believed to have a basis in the early Greek and Roman people. It is a type of ritual in which you will do it faithfully and with determination daily for nine days, hence the name. This sort of ritual and magic has been practiced around the world and through several different religions, making it a type of magic that is relatable for many different people.

This spell works thanks to the green candles that will represent the wealth that you are looking to achieve, while the white candle is a sympathetic representation of you. Beyond that, this spell will also use a traditional chant—it is a combination of all sorts of Magical traditions, drawing from them all to get the most power out of it as it attempts to communicate with the universe's energy once and for all.

You are, of course, free to alter the prayer during this spell—you can use any prayer that you have made up on your own, or that you may have found that you relate closer to. No matter what you choose to do, the point is for you to feel like you are able to project your own energy into the world, which you cannot do if you are too busy getting caught up in the idea of forcing yourself to use a chant that is bothering you for some reason. When you do make some changes to the chant, however, make sure you record it down for future reference and use.

This spell will require you to get a green and a white candle, as well as an essential oil. Cinnamon, sandalwood, patchouli, bergamot, myrrh, and ginger are all good choices for this spell—choose whichever one you have on hand, or choose the one that you prefer over the others.

First, it is time to consecrate the candle—as with the other money rituals, carving a money symbol into the green candle can help with effectiveness, and you could even carve a symbol for yourself into the white one, helping you really identify and align yourself with this magic. After carving, if you have chosen to do so, it is time to anoint your candle with the oil. As with other spells in which you are hoping to receive, you should start at the top and work your way down to the bottom as you rub the oil in.

While you are anointing your candle, you should be entirely focused on the money that you are hoping to attract. Visualize yourself as a magnet, with money flowing in from all around you, naturally attracted to you for your magnetic pole. As you do this, you should feel the powers of attraction building within yourself. Make sure you visualize how the money is coming to you, visualizing the specific amount if there is one—however, make sure this is realistic. The larger the sum you are attempting to receive and the less likely it is that you will be able to come across that kind of money, the less likely it is that the universe will provide—after all, it is difficult to suddenly stumble upon a random million dollars in the park. However, stumbling upon a random $20 that you needed for gas is far more realistic.

Place both of your candles atop the altar, roughly nine inches apart from each other. When you light them, start the following prayer:

"Money, Money, come to me.
In great numbers multiplied by three.
Provide for me and keep me healthy,
Do no harm, and forever shield me.
This I accept, so mote it be,
Money, Money, come to me."

After you have said this, blow out the flame, or use a spoon to put it out. You will repeat this process every day for nine days, with you placing the candles an inch closer together every single day. As you do this, you want to continue to visualize the money that you are hoping to receive and attract. By the ninth day, you should have the candles touching each other entirely and allow the candles to burn to completion. Dispose of your remnants in the way that you see fit and go into the world, emanating that attraction.

Chapter 7: Spells For Health, Luck, And Life Enhancement

With how busy adult life can be, everyone feels a little run down sometimes. It is difficult to get through life without ever encountering that exhaustion that comes along with trying to get by. After all, adulthood is a mess of responsibilities left and right, draining on you and forcing you to go through them one by one if you hope to remain employed gainfully, remain under a roof, and drive a car to get from point a to b. It becomes easy to neglect your health, accepting that you are going to live in stress and exhaustion. You may find that your life is normally draining, causing you to want to give up.

These feelings of malaise can be linked to depression and anxiety, and both of those can be felt in response to any sort of spiritual blockage that may come your way. This means then that you may find yourself struggling and suffering in silence, despite your best efforts to feel effective, successful, and healthy.

When you are feeling all out of sorts, there is little as soothing or relaxing as trying to remove this negativity from your life. Luckily, there are spells for that. You can banish the negativity that keeps you down, draining on your very psyche as you go through daily life. You can invoke spells that will involve the invitation of good luck, of expelling the negativity, and even of attracting a new job that may be able to help you. Of course, though, little is as fantastic or helpful when you are in a funk or having a bad day than an aura cleansing bath, followed by these spells that can help prime your body and mind to receive the blessings and good energy that is all around you in the universe. All you have to do is prime yourself to attract it.

Aura Cleansing Bath Spell

The first spell you will learn to do is how to create a powerful combination of herbs that can help you heal your aura, cleanse your soul, and prepare you to welcome all of the good luck that the universe has in store for you, so long as you open your mind and heart to it and accept the bounty as it has been offered. This is perfect for when you feel like you lack any legitimate confidence or power, and you may want to eliminate some feelings of anxiety that you are suffering from.

This bath will work by tapping into several potent herbs that will help you clear your mind and feel your energy healing. You will start with rue—a powerful healing herb that has been used for ages to protect from harm. It helps prevent attacks, both spiritual and psychic, and it can help ward off curses. Using rue in a bath encourages optimistic attitudes and welcomes and invites prosperity.

Rosemary is a second herb that you will utilize—regularly used in kitchen witchcraft in order to remove negativity from the kitchen, particularly in the foods or water being served. It helps trigger healing and self-love, as well as triggering desire and encouraging beauty.

The last of the wonder herbs we will be discussing for this bath is guinea hen weed—this may be tricky to locate, but the power is undeniable. This is a plant native to the Amazon and Caribbean—it has been used in shamanism to treat fever and alleviating anxiety, as well as to help bolster the immune system against anything that could be thrown your way.

In particular, this bath can be done at any time, but if you use it in tandem with a New Moon, you will be able to start the next Lunar Cycle purified and feeling clean and healthy.

This bath is quite simple to put together, and as you do so, you can cleanse your soul, allowing you to start attracting and absorbing positive energy or good luck.

To begin, start by bathing yourself—you need to take a shower first to make sure that you do not taint your herbal bath with dirt or oils from your day. Start with a clean slate—try to use neutral soaps that will not linger on your body after the fact. When you are done bathing, either allow yourself to air dry or use a towel. Put on a robe and move to the kitchen.

You will now boil four pots of water. Wait for it to reach a rolling boil and then turn off the burner or heat. With the water still over the burner for the residual heat, then add in your herbs. In particular, add in a sprig of rosemary and rue, and then three guinea hen weeds leaves. You will allow your mixture to linger over the heat, steeping for 30 minutes.

As you wait for the mixture, it is time to attend to your bathroom. Make sure it is clean and ready for you to spend some time there. Place a white candle in the bathroom and then go and retrieve the herbal mixture. You should strain out the herbs and then place the water itself into its own container. Return to the bathroom and light the white candle.

Now, get into your bath, which should be filled with water that is warm or hot (but comfortably so), and use the herbal mixture to rub over your body. You can place your hand into your jar and rub the liquid over yourself slowly, starting at your neck and working your way down as you do so.

As you rub the mixture over your body, envision yourself allowing your negative energy and pollutants seeping out, allowing the mixture to draw it in and absorb it as you rub it over your skin. Meditate as you feel the negativity emanating out of you, and once it finally removes from you, almost as if you have removed a leech or something else stuck to you, spend the time to self-reflect. What did you remove? Was it a negative thought about yourself? A negative opinion of yourself? Whatever it was, release it into the water.

Continue this process as you remove all of the negative energy from yourself. Envision it being absorbed and neutralized by your herbal mixture. When you feel lighter, and you are done in your bath, unplug the tub and allow the energy to drain down into the pipes, envisioning what they look like as they swirl around and disappear forever.

Now, get out of your bath and allow yourself to gently air dry if you can. If not, be gentle with a towel as you clean yourself. You should feel at peace and relaxed. Please note that this should not be used if you are pregnant—guinea weed hen should be avoided during pregnancy.

Any time you feel like you are in a funk or otherwise stuck in a negative mindset, you can use this to your own benefit, allowing yourself to purify your mind and release the negative feelings into the universe and away from you, allowing good energy and luck to flow inwards instead.

Bad Luck Repelling Spell

Have you ever felt like you were plagued with bad luck, no matter where you went? Maybe the bad luck seems to follow you, leaving you to wonder what you did to deserve such negative karma in the first place. Do not fret; you can make this negative energy and bad luck go away with a simple spell that will remove the negativity and allow yourself to be open once more to the positive energies that you desire in your life.

This spell requires you to cast a double-intention spell—you are effectively first intending to remove the bad luck from you, and then you are drawing the positive energy inward instead to replace it. This effectively opens you up to being on the receiving end of the universe's blessings while rejecting the negative energy once and for all, protecting you from it. You will use a green candle and salt, allowing you to clean away the negativity, and then use cinnamon to purify and attract good energy.

Begin by consecrating your green candle—set it up with an oil that resonates well with you at the moment, and carve any symbols that you may wish to influence or bless you. With your candle ready for you, you can place it onto your altar.

Around the green candle, you should create a circle around it, using a handful of salt. This salt should purify the area, creating a barrier between the candle and the outside world, absorbing the negative energy. With the salt around it, declare:

"Bad luck and negative energy, I demand that you leave me alone NOW."

You want to be as assertive as possible when you say this, commanding the energy around you to leave the area. Your voice creates vibrations in the air, and those vibrations can help you tackle the negative energy floating around you, and when you are firm and loud, you are able to begin pushing that negativity away.

Now, light the candle inside of the circle. Imagine all of that bad luck around you, seeing it as a smoke or a fog around you, or in some other form—whatever may resonate with you. Now, in the same assertive, dominant voice, state:

"Now, remove all adversity from me. Let it all dissolve."

You should now imagine that adversity, that bad luck that formed the fog around you fading away. The fog that you see in your mind's eye should literally start to dissipate away around you, allowing you to then release it back into the universe.

As that negative energy fades away, take the time to meditate to yourself. You want to continue to see that negativity in your mind-melting away, just like the fog. Imagine it burning away thanks to your candle, being erased and neutralized before it is then released back into the universe. Continue this process as you breathe, imagining the fog fading away more and more with each breath.

After about five minutes, or whenever your negative energy and problems that you could see in your mind's eye have disappeared, open your eyes, and take a sprinkle of cinnamon in your fingers. With a firm, commanding voice, state:

"Only positive energy and good luck are welcome to flow within me now."

As you do this, then you can sprinkle the cinnamon on top of the salt surrounding the candle. With the mixture of salt and cinnamon, you should start to imagine the good luck flowing your direction. Visualize that cinnamon attracting good luck your way, creating a new flow for you in which the positive energy follows it straight to you. If anything, even remotely negative pops into your mind, reject it and replace the thought with something positive, focusing entirely on the opportunities that you will have soon.

Now, continue to focus on your meditation, imagining the good energy in the universe flowing toward you as you watch the flame continue to burn, waiting for the candle to finish erasing itself once and for all. When the candle has finished burning, you can then dispose of the salt, cinnamon, and the candle remains. Either flush it into the toilet, allowing the salt to be taken by the element of water, physically removing the negative energy it had absorbed.

Armor Of Luck Spell

This spell will help you cast off negative energy, allowing yourself to create a sort of magical shield through the use of onion and salt. If you have been feeling down on your luck or like a magnet for all of the negativity around you, this spell can help you purify yourself and shed off that negativity.

Even if you do not feel like negative energy has been coming your way, you can still take the time to heal from the negativity through the protective nature of this spell. You can use it preventatively, ensuring that the negativity is unable to touch you. Effectively, this becomes an armor for you, allowing you to attract luck and allow it to penetrate that armor while rejecting and repelling any negative energy before it can wreak havoc on your life.

This spell works primarily because it uses sea salt and onions. The salt is a purifying agent—thanks to the fact that it has been found to be sterilizing, healing, and allows for the preservation of food, it is seen to be incredibly positive and powerful. It is associated with purification and protection around the world. In particular, you will be using sea salt, which is as natural as you can get it, but if you cannot get sea salt or do not have it, you can substitute it for pink Himalayan salt or Epsom salt—you need the salt to be coarse rather than the fine salt you would use at the dinner table.

Onions, on the other hand, are seen to ward off evil—they used to be given to warriors to protect them and give them strength, and they have been used for ages to purify and protect. Health spells of all kinds exist in the world, such as slicing an onion in half and allowing it to absorb the bacteria in the air.

Lastly, the use of a white candle draws it all together and purifies while also focusing the energy and bringing the Divine into your spell as you cast it.

Altogether, you need one onion, coarse salt, a glass of water, a photo of yourself, and a single white candle. Begin by consecrating and anointing your candle in any fashion that you see fit. You may choose to make it particularly protective, adding the proper oils and herbs that you are relating to at that moment.

After you have finished this process, or if you have chosen to skip the consecration, place the white candle on the center of your altar and light it. Place your photograph next to the candle and then place the onion on top of the photo.

With the placement set, you will then imagine your intentions, channeling them into the salt as you take a handful of it. Imagine yourself imbuing the salt with positive energy and the ability to shield the photograph and candle. Imagine that intention gathering into your palm, where you are holding the salt, and see in your mind's eye how that power flows straight into the salt, tempering it with your energy.

Now, spread the salt into a circle around the candle and photograph. As you do this, watch the candle's flame flickering. Imagine that the candle is burning away any negativity in the room, purifying it as you do so. Then, close your eyes and take a deep breath as you begin to meditate.

Focus your intentions on protection and gathering the necessary shield from any negative energy or intentions that may be floating around you. Imagine them approaching the candle, only to be literally repelled by the salt, bouncing off of the invisible barrier created by the salt.

As you envision this in your meditation, begin to speak your chant. Remember, you can always change up the chant to be more specific or more true to you in particular. In this instance, the chant that you will be using is:

"By the Powers of Nature,
Allow the Wind of Good Luck to approach me.
Allow this Blessed Circle Protect me.
Allow the Fire of this candle enlighten me.
Allow the waters of the Earth to guide me.
Now it has been done. So, mote it be."

At this point, you should close your eyes once more and continue to meditate on what you have just asked for. Really imagine the energy of the candle and the salt coming together, protecting your very body. Imagine a thin armor engulfing you and surrounding you. Then, blow out the candle and allow the energy to dissipate. As the energy of the candle and the protective circle fade away, notice how you feel your own protection still lingering around your body, shielding you from any future negativity.

Now, bury the remains of the spell into the ground in a garden or on the beach. Keep in mind that the salt may kill off your plants if you bury it in flowers.

Job Attraction Spell

Do you need a new job? Do you hate your current one? Maybe you simply want a promotion at your current job. No matter the situation, you can make it happen. You can attract a new job if you do this spell just before an interview. You can make it happen if you decide to apply for a new job. You can do it when you are filing for a promotion at work.

No matter the situation, if it involves some sort of shift in job, this spell is going to be helpful to you.

In particular, you want to cast the spell during the Waxing Crescent Moon—3 days right after the New Moon. When you do it at this point in time, you plant your intention into the universe right as the Moon is beginning to grow and develop—by planting it at this point in time, you will be able to encourage the Moon's energy to grow it for you, and with the Full Moon, just a few weeks later, you will find the intention has grown and developed into so much more than it used to be. It will manifest itself as grown like the moon.

If at all possible, with the timing of the Lunar Cycle, try to start this spell on a Sunday Evening. If you can't, make sure it is at least during the New Moon for the best results.

This spell will work because you use bay leaves to purify—they will cleanse and create the power that you need to clear out spiritual blockages that may hold you back from achieving your job. You will offer rice, encouraging and attracting the good luck that you would need for the fresh start that a new job generally represents. The sea salt in the circle will create the protection during the ritual to keep everything pure and untainted by negative energy that would otherwise work against you.

Lastly, you will use a green candle's power and energy to help you consecrate everything into a small bundle that you can carry with you for good luck during your interview process.

You will need a green candle, a handful of uncooked rice, sea salt, bay leaves, a sachet, a knife, and a dish.

Begin by creating a salt circle on your altar or on whatever surface you are using. This can also be done on the ground if you are sitting down—just instead of making a smaller circle, cast a circle that is large enough for you to sit inside. As you do this, imagine the negative energy leaving your space.

Taking the green candle in your hand, prepare it by carving your name into the side. Start with the first letter of your name closest to the wick and work your way down. Write your full name if you can, being as specific as possible with the universe. As you do this, imagine your end goal—you want a new job. Allow that thought to imbue the candle as you carve it, consecrating it with your newest intention for the universe.

Place the dish within the circle of salt, or if you have done this on the ground, place the dish in front of you. Light the candle in your hand and allow some of the wax to drip down onto the dish before quickly affixing the candle to the dish with the molten wax. You will have to act quickly before the wax can harden to ensure that it is stable. Keep in mind that you should keep everything flammable away from the circle at this point as you do not want to risk a fire if the candle happens to tip.

Into the dish, add first the handful of rice along the bottom. Then, place the three-bay leaves nicely on top, imagining the energy coming together to attract positive energy while the salt continues to repel the negative.

While the candle continues to burn, begin to chant to yourself:

"Oh, Mother Goddess, the Queen of Wisdom and Magic,
Please open your doors; keep them open during the day and the night.
Extend your hand in my favor and clear my way,
Gift me a new job
According to Your Divine Will.
By the Power of Three, so mote it be."

As you finish speaking, allow the candle to burn and let yourself settle into a meditative state. While you do, offer your thanks to the Goddess for her support and for being present with you when you needed her most. Then, blow out the candle and put away the knife and candle. Place the rice and leaves into your sachet and place it somewhere safe within your room, preferably somewhere that you will interact with, though also somewhere that others will not find.

After a week, repeat this chant to yourself, holding the sachet and imagining good energy coming down to support you and ensure that you are able to get the new job that you desire. Really imagine yourself getting this job with ease, allowing yourself to then act accordingly. If you do this process right, you should find good fortune will bless you, and you will hear back about a job soon.

Chapter 8: Forbidden Spells Of Black Magic

If someone walking down the street heard you mention Black Magic, you would find that the reaction you would get is incredibly negative—it has this image of being entirely negative and evil, bringing destruction and pain to everyone around. However, this is not true at all: Black Magic, like all great and powerful tools and powers within the world, are primarily neutral—they can be used for good or bad, depending on the intention. Some people may cast Black Magic to create a love spell or spell of protection. This is not necessarily evil, so long as it is not intended to harm other people.

What Is Black Magic?

If you have heard the paranoia that surrounds the evil eye and hexes, which greatly color the opinion of those around you and how they see Black Magic, you would understand why this sort of magic is so frowned upon by those who do not know better. The evil eye and jinxes and hexes are all forms of Black Magic, and they are absolutely intended to hurt other people. However, it does not have to be painful. Evil Black Magic may bring along with it pain, death, distress, or revenge, but it can also involve positive intentions.

Black Magic, essentially, is a negative force. However, that does not necessarily make it evil. For example, is it evil to reflect evil intentions back into the universe to protect yourself? You are using negative magic—you are repelling the energy away from yourself. This is Black Magic, and yet the intention behind it was pure. It was meant to be protective and keep yourself safe.

Black Magic involves the intervention of free will in some way—for example, when you rejected the negative energy, you subverted the other person's free will. You prevented him from harming you, effectively removing that choice from him.

How Does Black Magic Work?

Black Magic toward other people, then, involves forcing your own free will onto someone else, taking theirs away. When you are using Black Magic, you are taking away autonomy, which is something sacred that should never be interfered upon. This magic works through the subversion of another person's intention, creating chaos where it goes, depending on how it is used. Negative forces that act upon the universe, usually through the use of dark energy or the dark arts, can be seen as an example of this, directly separating white or pure magic from the dark magic we are discussing now.

Black Magic Spells:

We will go over a handful of Black Magic spells now, looking at how they work—particularly at three spells that are intended to be used to influence love itself. Considering just how sacred love is to people, this is entirely unproductive. Asserting your own free will over someone else to force their affections is manipulative and will backfire—you cannot force someone else to fall into love with you, and if the previously discussed love spells have failed to provide you with the result you were seeking, it is entirely possible that the person you were hoping to influence actually does not love you and you should leave it alone. However, it is still a good idea to understand these processes. If not to use, you can at least defend yourself from the influence of dark magic simply by knowing that it is out there and should be avoided to begin with. By understanding this process, you can protect yourself from the dark arts once and for all.

Break-up Spell

This first spell is designed to break up other people. It can be done when the individual that you love is in a relationship with someone else, either marriage or otherwise. When you are in a relationship with someone else, you are not likely to be open to an affair, after all. The easiest way than to influence that person is to cause them to break up with the other person. By breaking them up, then you can encourage them to go to you, or you can allow yourself to be the only interest in that person's life. By removing your primary competitor at that point in time, you will be able to ensure that you are actually able to get the end result you hoped for—attracting the other person on your own.

This spell will involve several different ingredients—you will want to accumulate a white and a black candle, sea salt, seven whole cloves, or clove oil if you do not have them, a knife, athame, or pin for carving candles, white clothing for yourself, vinegar, black paper, a photograph of the people you are trying to break up, a lemon, a sterile needle, black string, and seven nails.

This spell will be the most potent if you use it on the full moon, but if you simply cannot wait, any night will work.

Begin this spell by wearing white clothing. Even just a white t-shirt can help you with this process and aid in the destruction of the couple. Begin by casting a circle with the salt. Then, using your athame or pin, carve the Algiz Rune into the white candle. Now, anoint the white candle with the clove oil that you have gathered, or if you do not have the oil, stab the seven cloves into the candle. This will be your protection during the ritual, keeping you free from harm as you meddle in dark affairs. Light the candle, casting an intention of keeping you safe.

Now, anoint the black candle, using your vinegar, and then light that one as well.

With the candles lit, take the photograph, and using the knife, athame, or anything else, cut up the photograph, leaving only the faces of the couple and then take the piece of black paper in front of you. Take your lemon and rub it with vinegar before slicing it in half using your athame. Then, sprinkle the fruit with some salt and then use vinegar.

Now, take your sterile needle and prick your fingertip, drawing blood. You will place one drop of blood on both faces, and then take one of the pictures and place it on the lemon's bare fruit. Place a nail through the photo, securing it to the lemon as you do so. Then, repeat this process with the other picture onto the other lemon.

With the lemons in front of you, use the black candle and drip the wax from it onto each. As you do this, imagine the negative energy flooding toward them. Allow your negative feelings to flow toward the couple. Imagine them fighting and their relationship failing. Perhaps they cheat on each other or say things that hurt each other. Then, imagine the positive feelings when they finally do break up. Continue to channel your energy through the candle until you know that you are done. Trust your intuition; it will let you know when to stop. Then, it is time to say the following chant three times:

"Using the power of my mind
And without being kind
I pass this evil wave of energy
To cause you indefinite agony
Bring only pain
Your love will not remain
With the strength of my bloodstained fingertip,
Demolish this relationship
With the strength of my bloodstained fingertip,
Demolish this relationship
With the strength of my bloodstained fingertip,
Demolish this relationship!"

Then, place the candle down and put the lemon halves together while using the nails to affix them to each other before tying the lemon with string. Wrap the lemon in the paper and place it under your bed. Then blow out first the black candle and then the white candle.

The next day, you need to bury the package and the candle somewhere that the sunlight never reaches—

perhaps underneath a porch or a thick bush. Then, that night, allow the white candle to burn until it uses the entire candle.

Forced Love Spell

Sometimes, people feel jilted—they feel like they never found unconditional love, which they wholeheartedly believe they may deserve, and they will force the point, asserting their own will over that of the other person. However, this is dangerous, and the other person deserves their own free will, free of your own intervention. Nevertheless, let us look at how to use a forced love spell. In doing this, the other person will be convinced that he or she is entirely in love with you, entirely devoted to you.

This spell will require several ingredients—you will need a red, black, and purple candle, clove incense, and calamus, cinnamon, and myrrh oil. From there, gather 13 rose petals, either black or a very deep red. You will then need several strands of your own hair, and some of your own genital secretions on a cotton ball. For men, this is semen, which can be prepared up to two weeks in advance, and for women involves vaginal mucus on a cotton ball. Then, gather a photo of you, your lover, and a sterile needle. You will also need a red string, a cauldron, and something belonging to your lover.

This spell is best cast on a Full Moon.

This spell will involve you gathering all ingredients, casting a circle, and using clove incense for your own protection.

Then, anoint the candles using first the myrrh oil, then the cinnamon oil, and lastly, the calamus oil. Place them onto the altar and light each one. Now, set the photographs in front of you and begin with the red candle—drop seven drops of red wax onto your picture first, and then on your loved ones. At this point, think about your loved one and how you would feel if he or she was entirely in love with you. Allow your thoughts to create energy and imbue it through the candle and onto her photo. Repeat with the black, and then purple candles.

Then, place your wax-covered candles face to face with each other and use the string to tie them together. This can be rolled or folded, so long as the photos themselves are touching and tied by a string.

Now, place the photos into the cauldron.

Take your petals and drop calamus oil on each petal. Then, drop each petal into the cauldron while saying:

*"Your love is strong, your love is mine forever,
It creates a link, a bond too strong to ever sever."*

Now, take your sterile needle and prick your finger before dropping blood onto the cotton ball and place it into the cauldron. Then, place the cotton ball covered in genital mucous into the cauldron as well. Now, you need to mix in your own hairs into the cauldron and then the item that you took that reminded you of your loved one.

Place a few more drops of the oils into the cauldron, then drip some of the candle wax from all three candles into it as well. Focus entirely on the unconditional love flowing toward you, gifting you with it. Then, repeat your chant:

"Your love is strong, your love is mine forever,
It creates a link, a bond too strong to ever sever."

At this point, set everything in the cauldron on fire. Make sure that you are somewhere that will not cause problems if you are burning and preferably, do this outside where you will not set off smoke alarms. As you do this, you will release the energy out into the universe. When the items have finished burning, allow them to cool and then bury them, along with the candles, outside next to a tree.

Bring Back an Old Love Spell

This last spell is used to return an old lover. If you have lost an old lover that you desperately wish to have come back into your life, this is the spell to use. Of course, remember, this is a black magic spell, and it is dangerous and does take over your target's free will.

When you do this spell, you want to make sure that the person loved you at some point—you will be able to then encourage the other party to reignite old feelings and miss you. This is so powerful that you may find the other person intentionally seeking you out, rather than making you chase after him or her.

This spell will require you to gather the following: An organic chicken wing, a red candle, a sterile needle, some of your blood, thread, wooden matches, and one sheet of parchment paper.

To begin, start by lighting the candle using a wooden match. Make sure this is with a wooden match specifically and do not use a lighter. Take the chicken wing and use it to trace the name of your lover onto the parchment paper. Of course, you will not really see anything there, but that is okay. What you need is the motion of the writing, allowing you to know that it is there. Then, you must trace your own name right over the name of the lover. Then, using the red candle, drop seven drops of wax across the paper. Imagine you and your lover together once more, laying together and holding each other in an embrace.

Now, take the sterile needle and prick your finger. You will need three drops of blood onto the paper alongside the wax. During the time that you are dropping the wax and blood onto the parchment, make sure that you are focused on your ex-lover. Think about how much you loved your ex and how much you truly wish your ex would return to your side. You want to feel that desire building up as an energy that you can then use to send off into the universe.

Now, build up all of that energy into your lungs, imagining your pining desire filling them, and blow it out, extinguishing the candle and then say:
"Salima Ratiki Bustako"

You will now set the chicken inside the paper, wrap it up, and tie it in a little package, which you now need to bury somewhere outside. Take the candle with you and save it, and then when the next Full Moon arises, light the candle once more and allow it to burn itself out.

Should You Use Black Magic After All?

Black Magic itself is not inherently evil. It is incredibly powerful, which can then lead to it being incredibly dangerous to utilize, but it is not necessarily evil. It can be when used negatively, but that should not be a reason to never use it in the first place.

Everything exists in dynamics between two extremes that represent opposites—this is why we have both creation and destruction. Without destruction, you could not create and vice versa. Without old, there can be no young, and vice versa. Without wet, you cannot have dry. The concept is that one cannot exist without the other, and that is okay. Everything must have an opposite force that exists in order to balance everything out. This means that Black Magic is a necessary part of the world in order to have White Magic. Without this Black Magic, you could not possibly practice your own White Magic.

Think of the yin-yang symbol for a moment—you must have black and white to have perfect harmony, and this is the same with magic as well. This means that Black Magic is just as valid as White Magic, and because of that, there is no inherent reason to avoid it, so long as you are safe and respectful about the free will of other people, it can absolutely be a valid choice to use.

How can Destructive Magic Generate Love Spells?

Now, you may be wondering how magic that is inherently negative and destructive could possibly produce love spells—which is a valid point to raise. However, if everything exists in dichotomies, in which there are destruction and creation, of course, you can destroy love to create love. The human body is constantly destroying in order to create new processes. It is constantly destroying cells in order to create new ones. When you breathe, you inhale and exhale.

Just as there is the natural cycle in which there is birth, life, and death, you can see a similar pattern in love. Just because you have destroyed something does not mean that you cannot create from the ashes, allowing yourself to form something entirely different as a result of the processes.

Think about the phoenix—it dies and then is reborn in its ashes, looking nothing like it once did. This is what you are doing—you may be destroying love, particularly in that break-up spell, but you are also able to create new love, with you. Of course, everything will come to an end and be destroyed eventually—even the Great Sun will eventually reach its demise after it finishes burning itself. This means, then, that the destruction of Black Magic can absolutely generate Love Spells on its own in its own way.

How Black Magic Can Be Helpful

If everything must die to be reborn at some point, then, sometimes, it must be useful to hurry it along at some point. This is absolutely true—think about how you may have hesitations about letting go of a past relationship in which your partner abused you. You are stuck on him, and you know that you should not be, and yet you cannot possibly let go. Should that be allowed to burn out on its own before you are allowed to feel joy and move on in your life? Should you be forced to endure that suffering, that heartbreak, and that unwillingness to move on from your life, all because you are naturally inclined to miss what you loved for so long?

What if that could be sped along to allow you to move into what is truly a loving and deserving relationship? Should you still wait until you are no longer interested in your ex-partner, who hurt you? It would be useful to end that infatuation once and for all to allow you to heal yourself and move forward. In letting that relationship die once and for all, you open yourself up to positivity and the chance for a happier, healthier relationship. That relationship, then, would be your best bet at happiness, and it would be remiss to tell you to suffer in silence until you naturally get over the relationship. No—you should absolutely be allowed to let go.

Letting go of that process would involve Black Magic. Would you do it?

Many people would. Think of other situations in which you may consider destroying something to make space for new discoveries and success. Perhaps you may have a mental block that you need to let go of in order to allow yourself to finally move forward and toward the money and success that you know that you deserve. Maybe there are petty problems that are destroying a relationship that really should not be, and you choose to use Black Magic to eliminate that problem altogether.

Despite the fact that Black Magic is inherently destructive, that does not make it evil. After all, fire is inherently destructive, and it is the single-most commonly used element within this book. The Sun is destructive—it could blow up and destroy us all. However, it would be insane to suggest that the sun ought to be destroyed or banished for being a destructive force. Just because the sun can cause sunburn and occasionally even cancer does not mean that someone should figure out some way to launch a satellite into orbit that will block the sun's light, acting like a constant eclipse.

Keep in mind, if you do decide to use Black Magic, that it can create great and powerful changes in your life. It is powerful and sudden, and when it does suddenly change, it can cause some serious unintended consequences. Nevertheless, the power should absolutely be considered if you feel like you are ready to use them. Just as driving a car could be fatal if you make one wrong move does not discourage you from driving to work every day, you should not feel limited to avoid Black Magic because of the risk. Simply drive responsibly, so to speak, and be prepared. Perhaps even bring someone experienced along to guide you.

Conclusion

Thank you so much for reading through *Wicca Candle Magic!* Hopefully, as you read through this book, you learned as much as possible about using candles for the benefit of yourself and those around you. You were guided through the process of understanding which candles you should use in certain situations, as well as how you should use a candle in order to send your energy and intentions into the world. Through reading this book, you prepared yourself to better understand how to imbue the universe with your own energy in order to get what you wished for without harming anyone at all.

In using the candle, tapping into the beautiful, dangerous, destructive, and yet life-giving fire element, you are able to direct your intentions with ease—you can use this power to help you harness and focus your energy and intentions in order to really allow them to be released into the universe around you. In doing so, you can effectively then begin to influence the world around you. In sending out positive, living, beautiful intentions, you can then encourage the universe to send back positivity to you to fill in the gaps you have left behind. In repelling the negative energy from you, rejecting it, and not allowing it to impact you, you also make room for positive energy to return to you.

This is the disguise of good luck that so many people may assume others wear—it is not good luck to be able to attract positive energy. In fact, it is actually incredibly intentional. When you attract good luck, you are actually receiving back the positive intentions that you have sent out into the universe, and accordingly, you are able to better function thanks to the help of the universe.

The universe returns what you send to it, and if you are constantly sending out negative energy, you will attract that negativity. However, in cleansing and purifying yourself, you attract positive returns.

As you have read through this book, you developed the skills that would help you use candles for changing the way you project your energy, doing so in order to receive positivity, blessings, and good fortune from the great universe.

From here, you need to decide if you wish to continue exploring the Wiccan way of life. Do you want to learn how to cast other spells? Are you interested in learning more ritual and skills that you can use to continue to change your life for the better? If you are, then you may choose to look into Moon Magic, or another elemental magic. You may look into kitchen magic, herbal magic, crystal, magic, or choose any other element that is appealing to you. You will find that element that resonates with you, and when you do, stick to it, and hold onto it. By finding that element that resonates with you, you will find yourself having so much more luck and ease casting these spells around you. Now, if you found this book enjoyable, beneficial to you in any way, or generally interesting to you, please do not hesitate to provide a review on Amazon.

Reviews are crucial for a book to thrive on Amazon; otherwise it will simply die away. Hence our survival as authors and publishers heavily depends on them. So, if you found this book useful in any way, I would be delighted to see a review from you with a simple feedback on what you liked and what can be improved.

Thank you so much reading to the end of this book, and good luck on your endeavors in the world of magic!

Recommended Further Reading

Now, this book has ended, but that does not mean that you cannot be provided with other resources that could be beneficial to you in any way. In finding the proper resources, you can begin to develop an even more solid foundation into the Wiccan way of life, and in doing so, you may find so much more success in using magic in ways that will change your life for the better.

You may try looking into a forum in which people talk about everything from crystals to spells, from spirit guides to Books of Shadows: the form known as Everything Under the Moon will provide you to the collection and conglomeration of many, many different people's discoveries and experiences with their own Wiccan beliefs and opinions. They are there to speak to, and the forums are divided nicely into easily followed categories:

http://everthingunderthemoon.net/forum/

Beyond that, you may look into the website known as The Celtic Connection—this is incredibly straightforward and will provide you with a myriad of interesting and useful advice that you can use in order to get all of the knowledge that you need:

Https://wicca.com/

And of course, if you wish to read more of my books , just look for the following titles on Amazon:

- **Wicca For Beginners:**
  Your Practical Handbook of The Wiccan Path. Discover the Secrets of Wiccan Magick and Spells and How to craft Your Book of Shadows.
  - By Arin Corvinus

- **Wicca Moon Magic:**
  The Secret Lore Of Harnessing The Lunar Energy To Get What You Want – Including More Than 33 Lunar Spells And Rituals
  - By Arin Corvinus

Further Tables Of Correspondence

Anointing Oils By Purpose

Remember, to anoint a candle; you want to start at the top from the wick and down to the bottom in order to attract energy toward yourself. On the other hand, you want to go from the bottom up to the wick when you wish to expel or force something out.

When consecrating, you want to dip your fingers into the oil of your choice and then rub it along the whole surface. When you do this, you can dress the spell with herbs as well if you choose to do so.

- **Asserting Control:** Bayberry Oil
- **Boosting Energy:** Rosemary Oil, Peppermint Oil, Cinnamon Oil
- **Creating Balance:** Magnolia Oil
- **Divining:** Yarrow Oil, Myrrh Oil, Honeysuckle Oil, and Jasmine Oil

- **Dreams:** Jasmine Oil
- **Encouraging Healing:** Frankincense, Myrrh, Lavender, Clove, Cedar, Carnation, Gardenia Oil
- **Exorcising:** Yarrow, Dragon's Blood
- **Happiness:** Gardenia, Amber, and Bergamot Oil
- **Harmony:** Ylang-Ylang Oil, Gardenia Oil

Love Spells

Whenever in doubt or if you cannot get a hold of one of the love spell oils, you can always substitute for lavender or rose oil.

- **Attracting Love:** Patchouli, Gardenia, Frangipani, and Amber
- **Breaking Up:** Columbine Oil
- **Cause someone to fall in love:** Violet, Musk, Lavender, Jasmine
- **Create sexual love and lust:** Nutmeg, Orange, Musk

- **Encouraging Commitment:** Rose, Patchouli

- **Encourage someone to return to a lover:** Lavender oil (for you), Rose oil (for the other person)

- **Find true love:** Ylang-Ylang, Frangipani, Rose Oil

- **Fostering Faithfulness:** Magnolia Oil

- **Prevent divorce:** Lemon Oil

- **Improving Fertility:** Rose Oil

- **Influencing Creativity:** Peppermint Oil, Clove Oil

- **Money Attraction:** Vetiver, Peppermint, Jasmine, Heliotrope, Honeysuckle, Cinnamon, Bergamot Oil

- **Prosperity Attraction:** Musk Oil, Bayberry Oil

- **Protection:** Myrrh, Heliotrope, Pine, Patchouli, Carnation, High John the Conqueror, Lotus, Bayberry, Juniper, Rosemary, Dragon's Blood, Frankincense, Violet, Lilac

- **Purifying and Cleansing:** Sage Oil, Patchouli Oil, Frankincense Oil, Dragon's Blood Oil, Lotus Oil, Cedar Oil
- **Removal of Hexes or Curses:** Vetiver, Myrrh, Dragon's Blood, Cedar, Yarrow
- **Strength:** Carnation Oil

Color Correspondence:

In the absence of the correct color of candle, you can use white as a sort of all-purpose candle instead, though having the correct color is always preferred.

- **Black:** Absorption, accepting reality, anger and anger management, death, the Afterlife, rebirth, banishing, releasing, negativity, challenges, binding, determination, loss, endings, the breaking of hexes, grief, magic, persistence, patience, secrets, self-control, karma, spirituality

- **Blue:** Interviews, study, marriage, sleep, justice, career, leadership, wisdom, pregnancy, mental obstacles, dreams and sleep, honesty, trust, mental challenges, communication, trust

- **Brown:** Protection, grounding, endurance, finding the lost, providing courage and balance, hard work, animals, the material world, stability

- **Green:** Peace, harmony, healing, abundance, luck, action, creativity, acceptance, action, the environment, luck, family, fertility, change, beauty, abundance, prosperity, nurturing

- **Gold:** The God and Sun Magic, masculine energy, abundance, positivity, money, happiness, ambitions, fortune, power, divination, creativity, influence, luxury

- **Orange:** Travel, stimulation, vitality, discipline, abundance, freedom, adaptability, ambition, justice, goals, freedom, independence, creativity, confidence, pleasure, positive energy, strength, courage, celebration, money

- **Pink:** Family, fidelity, children, passion, sensuality, marriage, love, affection, acceptance, compassion, femininity, friendship healing from abuse, kindness, reconciliation

- **Purple:** Addiction, authority, astrology, emotions, enlightenment, independence, influence, imagination, power, overcoming fear, truth, spirituality, writing, wisdom, psychic protection, spiritual development,

- **Red:** Assertiveness, action, business, creativity, desire, energy, loyalty, love, change, overcoming challenges, passion, motivation, strength, romance, survival

- **Silver:** The Goddess and Moon and Star Magic, awareness, feminine energy, fertility, hidden potential, divination, healing, intuition, money, stability, success, psychic powers, purification, the ocean,

- **White:** Attraction, balancing, cleansing, bringing clarity, divination, healing, guidance, grounding, hope, higher self, peace, optimism, innocence, truth, spirituality, workplace magic, willpower, protection

- **Yellow:** Action, business, credit and loans, communication, friendships, happiness, learning new skills, intellect, inspiration, knowledge, travel, inspiration, intuition, stimulation